THE BBC TV SHAKESPEARE
Literary Consultant: John Wilders

THE MERCHANT OF VENICE

THE BBC TV SHAKESPEARE

THE BBC TV SHAKESPEARE

Literary Consultant: John Wilders
Fellow of Worcester College, Oxford

The Merchant of Venice

BRITISH BROADCASTING CORPORATION

Published by the
British Broadcasting Corporation
35 Marylebone High Street
London W1M 4AA

ISBN 0 563 17856 6

This edition first published 1980
© The British Broadcasting Corporation
and The Contributors 1980

The text of the Works of Shakespeare
edited by Peter Alexander
© William Collins Sons and Company Ltd 1951

The text of *The Merchant of Venice* used in this volume is the Alexander
text, edited by the late Professor Alexander and chosen by the BBC as the
basis for its television production, and is reprinted by arrangement with
William Collins Sons and Company Ltd. The complete Alexander text is
published in one volume by William Collins Sons and Company Ltd under
the title *The Alexander Text of the Complete Works of William Shakespeare*.

All photographs are BBC copyright (David Green)

Printed in England at
The Pitman Press, Bath

CONTENTS

PREFACE

John Wilders

The precise year in which Shakespeare wrote each of his plays and the order in which he composed them is not known, but it is likely that *The Merchant of Venice* was written in about 1597, shortly after *A Midsummer Night's Dream* and immediately before *Henry IV Part 1*. The stories which provide the two main plots are both very ancient. The tale of the pound of flesh was originally an eastern folk-tale which began to appear in written form in the twelfth century, but the version which Shakespeare used was probably the one included in a collection of prose tales called *Il Pecarone* ('The Dunce'), written by Ser Giovanni Fiorentino and published in Italy in 1558. The tale of the three caskets is equally ancient and was a popular myth before it was put into writing in the ninth century. Shakespeare could have found it in Boccaccio's collection of short stories, *The Decameron*, but his most likely source was another anthology, the *Gesta Romanorum*, first published in English in 1577.

There is a tradition that Shylock was first played by Shakespeare's fellow actor Richard Burbage and that he portrayed him as a figure of fun. This comic interpretation seems to have persisted until 1741 when Charles Macklin departed from tradition and presented him as a ferocious and terrifying villain. Early in the following century Edmund Kean became the most celebrated Shylock of his age and added greatly to the range of emotions he conveyed, but it was not until Sir Henry Irving took on the role in 1879 that he was portrayed as a movingly tragic figure, the dignified victim of religious persecution. During the twentieth century there have been distinguished performances by Michael Redgrave, Emlyn Williams and Peter O'Toole in England and George C. Scott in the United States. Laurence Olivier played the role under the direction of the producer of this television series, Jonathan Miller. This television production, directed by Jack Gold, was recorded at the BBC Television Centre in May 1980.

INTRODUCTION TO
THE MERCHANT OF VENICE

John Wilders

Shakespeare created *The Merchant of Venice* by adapting and combining two existing traditional stories: the tale of the heiress who can be won only by the choice of one of three caskets, and the tale of the malevolent usurer who tries to murder his debtor by cutting away a pound of his flesh. Both tales were already very ancient and had been told many times before Shakespeare wove them together in this one play. When combined they contain the ingredients of what could have been a thoroughly conventional romantic comedy: a rich, beautiful and intelligent heroine; a young, handsome, eligible hero; and a villain whose animosity casts a temporary cloud over their marriage.

In adapting these stories for the stage, however, Shakespeare created a play which is far from simple or conventional, for he gave to the characters a complexity – even obscurity – of motivation which did not exist in the original versions. We have no doubt about how Shakespeare's characters act but we are constantly left uncertain as to why they act, and this sense of uncertainty is created by the very first scene, where we are invited to consider Antonio. Indeed in his opening speech Antonio admits that he himself is baffled by his own state of mind:

> In sooth, I know not why I am so sad.
> It wearies me; you say it wearies you;
> But how I caught it, found it, or came by it,
> What stuff 'tis made of, whereof it is born,
> I am to learn;
> And such a want-wit sadness makes of me
> That I have much ado to know myself.

The affectionate, concerned young merchants who are his friends offer various reasons for Antonio's dejection: one believes that he is anxious for the safety of his ships, another that he is in love, and

8

a third – Gratiano – mockingly suggests that he puts on the appearance of solemnity in order to be thought wise. In view of the peril in which he later finds himself it may be that his sadness is a premonition of disaster, but, since the true cause is never disclosed, we have no means of knowing.

As the scene develops, however, Shakespeare hints at another possible explanation if we choose to find it. The friendship between Antonio and Bassanio is shown to be a very intimate one. Bassanio confesses that to Antonio he owes the most 'in money and in love', and Antonio, in turn, assures Bassanio that his 'purse, person and extremest means' are all at his disposal. It also appears that Bassanio is about to desert his friend and go in quest of a wife, and, indeed, the wooing of Portia is the first subject Antonio mentions when the two men are left alone. His sadness may, therefore, arise from Bassanio's imminent departure and possible marriage. This in itself would be of no great significance did it not, in due course, reflect on the motives behind Antonio's offer to stand surety for Bassanio's loan from Shylock. To give money freely to a friend, as Antonio has evidently done in the past, or to offer to stand surety for a loan, as he now proposes to do, places an obligation – not a financial, but a less tangible moral obligation – on the recipient. Although in wooing Portia Bassanio is attempting to break free of the bonds of friendship and replace them with the bonds of marriage, Antonio is nevertheless keeping a hold on him by imposing on him a debt which can be repaid only by loyalty. The bond of loyalty which ties Bassanio to Antonio is not broken even when the former has crossed the sea to Belmont. In fact Bassanio is made to feel this obligation when, immediately after he has won his bride, he hears from Venice that Antonio's ships have been wrecked and that Shylock is threatening his life. No sooner has he pledged himself to Portia than he feels his moral debt to Antonio pulling him away from her:

> I have engag'd myself to a dear friend,
> Engag'd my friend to his mere enemy,
> To feed my means.

The words of Antonio's letter serve merely to tighten the bond which links Bassanio to him:

> Since . . . it is impossible I should live, all debts are clear'd between you and I if I might but see you at my death. Notwithstanding, use your pleasure; if your love do not persuade you to come, let not my letter.

Antonio, we are told, 'loves the world' only for the sake of Bassanio. His apparent selflessness in standing surety for his friend turns out, paradoxically, to be the means whereby he binds Antonio to him, as Portia perceives:

> First go with me to church and call me wife,
> And then away to Venice to your friend;
> For never shall you lie by Portia's side
> With an unquiet soul.

If, at this point in the play, we reconsider the opening scene, we may question how far Antonio's apparent liberality was an indirect or unconscious form of possessiveness.

A baffling mixture of motives also seems to lie behind Bassanio's decision to try and win Portia as his wife. When asked by Antonio about the lady he intends to woo, he replies not by describing Portia but by reminding Antonio of his impoverishment and declaring his intention to recoup his losses by embarking on a new financial venture. It is in this context that he introduces the subject of Portia:

> In Belmont is a lady richly left,
> And she is fair and, fairer than that word,
> Of wondrous virtues.

Although Bassanio is not unaware of Portia's natural endowments, it is in her wealth that he is primarily interested. He will, as he explains, try to win her because his 'mind presages . . . thrift' (or 'profit'), and, indeed, once he has gained her he finds her as generous in her offer to pay off his debt to Shylock as Antonio had been to finance his expedition. In the event, of course, Shylock refuses to be bought off with money and Portia is compelled to save Antonio by exercising the 'wondrous virtue' of her intelligence. But in successfully thwarting Shylock's intentions, she also manages to bind Bassanio even more closely to herself, no longer simply as his wife but as the redeemer of his dearest friend.

Bassanio's double obligation to Portia becomes apparent at the end of the episode involving his gift to the supposed lawyer of his wife's ring. When asked by the disguised Portia, at the conclusion of the trial, to hand over the symbol of his recent marriage, Bassanio once more finds himself caught between two conflicting duties: his obligation to his wife, to whom he has sworn to keep the ring, and his gratitude to the saviour of his friend, to whom Antonio stands indebted 'in love and service evermore'. In handing over the ring he is conscious of breaking his oath to Portia, and his consequent sense of guilt is only removed when wife and lawyer turn out to be one and the same person. Whereas the play began with the cementing of Bassanio's bond of friendship with Antonio, it ends with the strengthening of his bond of marriage to Portia. 'Pardon this fault,' he begs his wife,

> and by my soul I swear
> I never more will break an oath with thee.

As though to point out the parallel between the opening and the closing of the play, Antonio then adds,

> I once did lend my body for his wealth,
> Which, but for him that had your husband's ring,
> Had quite miscarried; I dare be bound again,
> My soul upon the forfeit, that your lord
> Will never more break faith advisedly.

As the couple finally leave the stage for their marriage bed, Antonio is left alone and, although it is difficult to decide how much Shakespeare intended us to be aware of the merchant's solitude, we can, if we wish, notice that his hold on Bassanio is now broken.

Shylock, as a usurer, deals professionally in bonds of a more literal and legal kind, and has a better understanding of their power. In making the, for him, exceptional offer of a loan free of interest, but in return for the promise of a pound of flesh should the money not be repaid, he claims to be acting out of generosity. 'I would be friends with you, and have your love,' he assures Antonio, and the latter, at least, believes him, recognising as he does so that a free loan is, indeed, a means of 'buying favour'. After the wreck of Antonio's ships, however, the 'merry bond' which Shylock had proposed ostensibly as a sign of peace becomes the means whereby he may make an attempt on the merchant's life. His initial expression of supposed friendship, like Antonio's initial gesture of love, enables him to exercise greater power over the recipient.

Shylock's true motives for proposing the bond are, of course, not generous at all, as the audience well knows, for he tells them in an aside that he hates Antonio because 'he is a Christian',

> But more for that in low simplicity
> He lends out money gratis, and brings down
> The rate of usance here with us in Venice.

The Jew's animosity towards the Christian is, however, understandable because the latter has provoked it, as Shylock sharply points out:

Signior Antonio, many a time and oft
In the Rialto you have rated me
About my moneys and my usances;
Still have I borne it with a patient shrug,
For suff'rance is the badge of all our tribe;
You call me misbeliever, cut-throat dog,
And spit upon my Jewish gaberdine,
And all for use of that which is mine own.

Antonio, far from denying these accusations, admits that he will go on persecuting Shylock as before:

I am as like to call thee so again,
To spit on thee again, to spurn thee too.

At this point in their conversation it is difficult to know which of the two is the more culpable, Antonio for his inhumanity towards Shylock or Shylock for his consequent hatred of Antonio. Hence, when the latter stands in the courtroom exposing his flesh to the edge of Shylock's knife, we again find it difficult to decide which of the two is the more guilty party, Antonio for persecuting Shylock or Shylock for trying to get his revenge. Religious persecution is perhaps preferable to attempted murder, but a firm, simple judgement cannot be made. Yet the situation takes place in a court of law where judgement one way or the other cannot be avoided.

The responsibility for deciding the case rests, as it turns out, in the hands of Portia, and her first, shrewd and humane impulse is to avoid the necessity for judgement by appealing to Shylock's mercy. Had she succeeded she would have saved not only Antonio but, as we later realise, Shylock from the justice of the court. Both she and the Duke attempt repeatedly to dissuade Shylock from taking the pound of flesh to which he is legally entitled, by offering him more than the original sum, by appealing to his humanity, and by delaying the fatal moment with enquiries about the scales and the need for a surgeon. But he is adamant. What he fails to realise is that, in rejecting her pleas and persistently demanding the enforcement of justice, Shylock is unwittingly ensuring his own absolute defeat. Having turned the law against him by insisting that he shed no blood, Portia goes on to forbid not only the payment of three times the capital which Bassanio had offered him but the original sum itself and, by the time he makes his crestfallen exit from the court, Shylock finds himself deprived of half his goods and of the religious faith by which he had governed his life. The bond which the Jew had drawn up in order to avenge himself on the Christian produces the opposite result to the one he had intended. Designed to deprive Antonio of his life, it deprives Shylock of 'the means whereby he lives'.

In having to adjudicate between Shylock and Antonio, both Portia and the court are placed in a situation where no wholly satisfactory judgement can be made. Shylock has the law on his side and Portia rightly refuses to flout the law. But had she allowed Shylock to kill his victim in open court we should obviously not have found her judgement satisfactory. Nor, however, can we unreservedly approve the outcome of the trial as it stands. In spite of his mercenary preoccupations, the violence of his hatred towards Antonio, and the unconstrained relish with which he holds the merchant in his power, Shylock is at the same time an often sympathetic figure and certainly the most powerfully living character in the play. His antipathy towards Antonio, as we have seen, has strong justification, especially when he associates himself with generations of Jews, his 'sacred nation', who have endured persecution by the Christians. 'Suff'rance' has, indeed, been the badge of all his tribe. The gentiles in the courtroom no doubt feel that, by requiring him to become a Christian, they are doing him a favour, compulsorily enabling him to save his soul. But for Shylock this must seem a final, cruel penalty exacted by a Christian majority which has always persecuted him. The audience are allowed to see both points of view and find them irreconcilable, not knowing where to place their sympathies.

This uncomfortable effect is sustained into the last act in which the Christians, preoccupied as they are with their reunion in Belmont, the problem of the rings and the news that Antonio's ships are safe, give no thought at all to Shylock whom they mention only once, and then as the enforced benefactor of Lorenzo and Jessica. It is unlikely that the audience, however, will so easily forget the ominous figure of Shylock whose defeat they have just witnessed, and we may wonder how far Shakespeare intended their disregard of that ruined man to be a silent comment on their frivolity. The dramatist may or may not invite us to read between his lines.

To the interwoven stories of the pound of flesh and the three caskets, Shakespeare added two sub-plots, both of which again raise awkward questions about bonds and the conflict of loyalties. As Bassanio allows his friendship with Antonio to be superseded by his marriage to Portia, so Jessica deserts her father and absconds with his money in order to marry Lorenzo, an act which arouses in us those mixed feelings characteristic of this play. On the one hand we learn, from the few hints Shakespeare supplies, that Shylock is a cheeseparing housekeeper and a tyrannical father who forbids his daughter so much as to look at the antics of the irresponsible Christians. To that extent we can sympathise with her impulse to escape to freedom with her lover. On the other hand we can also see the effect of her elopement on Shylock, who feels affronted that his own 'flesh and blood' should abandon him. In the scene in which he first bewails the loss of his ducats and his daughter and then gloats over Antonio's losses, he appears by turns pathetic, vindictive and bizarre, but the impression we receive of Jessica through him is of a heartless and trivial girl who has little thought for her father's feelings or his property. Her brief, hasty reference to Shylock is scarcely a token gesture towards family loyalty:

> if my fortune be not crost,
> I have a father, you a daughter, lost.

She compares unfavourably with Portia who obeys the instructions of her dead father to the letter even though they limit her freedom. Jessica's gain is shown to be Shylock's tangible loss and she scarcely senses the effect her elopement will have on him. Once again it is hard to judge which of the two is the more culpable.

Launcelot Gobbo, on the other hand, in his comic exposition of a similar choice, is at least aware that he is in a moral dilemma. He recognises that duty and conscience compel him to remain loyal to his master, Shylock, yet he also believes that to remain faithful to a Jew is to serve 'a kind of devil':

> Certainly the Jew is the very devil incarnation; and, in my conscience, my conscience is but a kind of hard conscience to offer to counsel me to stay with the Jew.

In his inward struggle between domestic and religious scruples, he decides to offer his services to Bassanio, not because this is clearly the right course of action, for in doing so he obeys what he calls the voice of 'the fiend', but because that is where his own best interests lie: Shylock is a frugal housekeeper but Bassanio 'offers rare liveries'. As Shylock is abandoned first by his servant, then by his daughter, he consoles himself with his one hope, which is the defeat of Antonio. When that fails he appears to have neither means not motive to survive and his last words, 'I am not well', sound chillingly ominous.

By combining these several plots into a single play, Shakespeare wrote what is a romantic comedy only in the outlines of its story. Moreover, in his frequent references to the deceitfulness of outward, surface appearances, he seems to invite us to look more deeply into it:

So may the outward shows be least themselves.

Not only do the various bonds or agreements in which the characters casually engage themselves turn out to have more serious effects than they had foreseen, but the play itself raises more worrying problems than its surface leads us to expect. The characters repeatedly find themselves forced to choose between conflicting obligations: Bassanio between the ties of friendship and those of marriage, Portia between her duty to her father and her natural desire to choose herself a husband, Shylock between the claims of justice and those of mercy, Jessica between her obligation to Shylock and her desire for money, love and freedom, Gobbo between the voice of 'conscience' and the temptations of 'the fiend'. Indeed, the central dramatic episodes all portray moments of choice, as Portia's suitors in turn assess the significance of the three caskets and she herself determines the fates of Antonio and Shylock in the courtroom. The one characteristic which all these situations share in common is that they admit of no wholly satisfactory solution: in giving Portia's ring to the lawyer Bassanio betrays his wife's trust and in saving Antonio Portia at the same time ruins Shylock. It can be no accident that, as Lorenzo and Jessica wait idly at Belmont for Portia's return, their conversation (which could have been about all kinds of things) is about lovers whose loyalties have been betrayed: Troilus by Cressida, Dido by Aeneas, and Shylock by his faithless daughter.

So frequently is this idea repeated that Shakespeare seems to assume that insoluble dilemmas and unavoidable betrayals are an inescapable part of the human condition and this idea is underlined by the occasional comments on the frailty and corruption of human nature. Thus Portia:

If to do were as easy as to know what were good to do, chapels had been churches, and poor men's cottages princes' palaces. It is a good divine that follows his own instructions.

And, on her return from Venice, seeing the light of home and thinking, possibly, about the drama in which she has just been engaged:

How far that little candle throws his beams!
So shines a good deed in a naughty world.

The one idea of perfection invoked in this play is that of the abstract, divine expression of music, especially the transcendent music of the spheres which, however, is so perfect that it cannot be heard by the mortal, corrupted senses of men. 'Such harmony', says Lorenzo,

is in immortal souls,
But whilst this muddy vesture of decay
Doth grossly close it in, we cannot hear it.

In the imperfect world Shakespeare portrayed in *The Merchant of Venice* few, if any, actions are wholly good and few, if any choices are between the absolutes of right and wrong. Beneath the surface of this immensely popular comedy we can find, if we choose to look for them, ideas which are not comic at all.

THE PRODUCTION

Henry Fenwick

At first sight Jack Gold might seem a surprising choice of director for a television production of *The Merchant of Venice*. Well known and highly praised as the director of television programmes such as *The Naked Civil Servant* and films like *Aces High*, he happily admits to having no Shakespearian experience at all. 'One thinks of Jack primarily as a person who brings a trmendously vigorous and efficient and interesting imagination to bear on modern subjects', his producer, Jonathan Miller, acknowledges. 'Working with something like *The Merchant of Venice*, I think it will roughen the grain of the work to have him not planing smoothly and complacently along the lines of traditional assumptions.'

Gold himself points out that his past work has not been exclusively modern, but he confesses that tackling Shakespeare was something of a major step for him. 'I was getting to the stage of finding the sort of films I was doing – not difficult,' he says (he shies away from actually saying 'easy'). 'That may sound arrogant but it's not. If you do something long enough, you actually do find you know what you're doing. They were taxing up to a point but they didn't take me into whole new areas. I felt my mind needed stretching. Shakespeare was a great way of stretching myself, both with the play and actually by working in the studio.' (Surprisingly enough, Gold has done very little television studio work.) 'I stretched myself two ways and had a marvellous time.'

Though he had never worked on a Shakespeare play before Gold had, he says, seen plenty of productions 'and the thing that always gets me is that I so rarely understand what they're talking about! I know that they're using English words, but the language is so different from the language we use now that I made it a prime element to understand what the characters were saying. I knew that if people understood what they were saying then the verse would follow, but if you went for the verse only – and you can get very high on speaking Shakespeare, because it *is* very beautiful and, though not all *The Merchant* is in verse, of course, you can get

17

high just on the language – very often the meaning gets lost. The actors seem to fly away in the language and forget that there are a lot of people who do find the language a barrier.

'What I did totally try to do was to avoid the feeling that there was a poetry reading going on. These were *characters* who spoke to each other; and the fact that the language is marvellous doesn't mean to say that it is anything other than *dialogue*. There are certain scenes, like "On such a night", the exchange in the Belmont garden between Lorenzo and Jessica, when you know it, you know that it's some of the most beautiful poetry ever written. But it's *not a poetry contest*. They happen to be two realistic characters, so I turned it into a sexual contest and made it quite – well, not sexually explicit, but getting that way – so it becomes a love conversation rather than a poetry competition. The fact that they speak poetry to each other is marvellous, but they're two people who have just eloped and have probably been making love to each other non-stop ever since and can't wait to get each other back into bed. That may be wrong but it certainly seemed to make two living characters there, speaking dialogue to each other!

'I'd only worked in the television studio really properly once before, on a Play of the Month, *Mario*, an Isaac Babel play, and that had a naturalistic set. Having read *The Merchant* I thought: this is not about sitting down and about props. It's about people speaking to each other, relating to each other. It's also a very dynamic piece: I could see it with a lot of movement. So in order to make it easy for myself I had an idea of virtually turning the studio into a location: designing a set so that no matter in what direction you pointed the camera you'd always be in Venice or in Belmont.'

The solution worked out with designer Oliver Bayldon was to create two 360-degree backcloths, one for Venice, one for Belmont. The final results look like two overwhelming impressionistic landscape paintings, each of which, on different days of shooting, completely line the walls of the huge studio. Working out these backcloths was quite a difficult process, and Bayldon showed me a couple of small rough drafts on boards, miniature paintings he had done before putting his team to work painting the enormous gauzes. 'I did quite realistic versions to begin with, then gradually obliterated the realistic details bit by bit,' he recalls. 'Belmont was to be airy, Venice earthy. I worked in blue-grey and reddish ochre colours'. As reference for his drafts of the cloths he turned to Canaletto, Turner, 'some shades of Piper, too, though it may not be evident – an odd mixture, really. Monet crept in too, of course.' The Belmont cloth represents the great garden of Belmont, stretching apparently into the distance. 'Jack, or perhaps it was Jonathan, said that it should be mountainous because that's what Belmont means, but I must confess that went by the way a bit. I went for atmosphere – firs and pines against an enormous sky, lots of sky, the horizon goes on a long way: blue and distant. Behind the cloth there was a white cyc and the light goes through the gauze and bounces off the cyc, so there's white light bouncing back through it all the time and it's very softened and blended. Venice was less classical in feeling, a strong element of the medieval. I used ochre and tan, almost a monochrome.' The Venice cloth, again totally impressionistic, stretches around the studio, conveying, in its blurred outlines, seascape, then bridge, then a dense collection of buildings – the ghetto area where Shylock lives.

The actual painting of these cloths posed something of a problem: their size meant that each had to be painted in three sections in the workshop. Since different people were working in shifts on the sections, maintaining consistency of style as each section was finished and its adjoining section begun became a major worry; but Bayldon's original miniatures seem to have proved adequate models.

The architectural details that were to be placed in front of the backcloth in the middle distance of the shots were slightly more realistic in style, though still not wholly so: columns, a couple of arches, steps to form a bridge, elements 'like enormous triangular cheese wedges', each side painted slightly differently, and everything on castors, easily movable. For Belmont there was the more permanent detail of a gazebo, at first designed to be Palladian, classical pillars and a solid domed roof: 'then Jack said, "I'm going to have a lot of action under this – how am I going to light it?", so at that point it couldn't be anything solid.' Instead of a domed pavilion, therefore, the gazebo design became rather airier – modelled very loosely on a photograph found in *Country Life* of a rather Edwardian folly, a curlicued Temple of Atalanta, much modified for the context of the play.

Bayldon confesses to having been extremely nervous when the time came to bring all these set elements into the studio. 'Until we got it in I didn't know what it would look like really; at one point I wasn't sure it was going to work. I walked in on the first day, while they were setting up. The gauzes were still on the floor, there was no floor paint down, nothing seemed to tie up; and I thought if

Jack had walked in then . . . But suddenly it all jelled!'

As it was, Jack was delighted with the freedom the sets gave him. 'I used the sets with an enormous amount of freedom and usually on single cameras. I could do long tracking shots right across the studio if I wanted to, it really was like being on location in Venice, though there was no pretence that we were in a real place. Occasionally there are scenes like the trial scene where I have several cameras going at once, but a lot of it was done with one camera and the actors working in relation to the camera, with everybody moving. The actors were almost always in the foreground: there is an optimum distance, it seems to me, for seeing actors in Shakespeare. Understanding the language is the most important thing: if they're too far away you don't hear, and if they're *too* close you don't hear. If you imagine different planes, the thing closest to the camera was the reality of the actor in a real costume – the costumes were totally real and very beautiful – then beyond the actor is a semi-artificial column or piece of wall, and in the distance is the backcloth, which is impressionistic.'

Raymond Hughes designed the 'very real' costumes, and for him, as well as for Oliver Bayldon, it was his first Shakespeare. 'It is a much larger play than I thought it was,' he says now. 'I thought it was one of his smaller works but I've got *sixteen* rails of costumes. There are twenty principal characters, when you come to count them up; it takes place over three months. Venice was very solid, Belmont very airy, on an almost ethereal plane, and change of mood and change of time is invariably done with costume.'

The subtlest difficulty, he found, was in differentiating character and place while still maintaining a consistency to bind class and kin. 'Bassanio, for example, should appear solid in Venice and ethereal in Belmont, but he's the same rank in both places; he's dressing up to go to Belmont as one would to go to court, but that change should never be experienced as a hiccup. Jessica's final dress in Belmont must be gorgeous, but she's not the same rank as Portia and mustn't seem to be. Venice was Titianesque in colour; we limited it to blacks and oranges, burnt umbers and those lovely greens Titian used – that was for the moody, gloomy sections of the play. Belmont is very much light and air, almost like Illyria, so we made it blue – more Canaletto in feeling, almost Watteau, though that's the wrong period of course, and all in soft focus. You know your're in somewhere quite different, it's a different play there, and we were allowed to mind-blow!' He chuckles at the freedom such a brief gave him. 'It *had* to be sumptuous; I felt that the set was there to put things in front of. The play is magical and, if you're slightly less than scintillating, you fail!'

There was no cutting of the text. 'I didn't touch a syllable,' says Gold. 'Maybe I'm wrong but I didn't feel any reason to. I did go through it thinking "Which bits are boring?", then I thought if it's boring it must be me, because everything seems to add another facet to the play. I suppose there are little scenes that could be cut out but it just seems unnecessary. I gave Shakespeare the benefit of the doubt and thought: they're there for a reason and I have to find a way of making them work.

'I'd only seen the play once before and that was only several months ago. The thing that hit me first was that there was no way, it seemed to me, of avoiding the racial element in it. No matter what you do it is *there*. When I read the play it seemed to me that one shouldn't avoid it, but also you can't avoid twentieth-century sensibilities and susceptibilities. So it becomes a matter of trying to find out *why* Shylock behaves the way he does. Starting from just looking at all the characters, you find they are *all* a mixture of black and white; all greys. Shakespeare has a marvellous awareness of human nature, knows that there is no reason why Hitler shouldn't love children, in effect. The fact that a man or woman may react to one person one way in a situation doesn't mean they can't react in what seems to be the opposite way in another situation. All the characters in the play, except maybe Nerissa, seem to have this mixture of elements. Antonio is a man who loves Bassanio, but despises Shylock as a Jew. Bassanio is a mixture of mercenary motives and high romantic love for Portia. Portia, who has been described as a saint, has reactions about dark-skinned gentlemen in her attitude to the Prince of Morocco: when she says, "Let all of his complexion choose me so", there's nothing unaware of colour in that situation. Gratiano is appalling to Shylock but to his friends he's a nice, open, honest extrovert. Does Lorenzo love Jessica for what she is or for the money she'll be bringing him? And Jessica – you never see Shylock behave badly to her and it's almost impossible to find elements in the play where he does. She has only one scene with him and all he does is warn her to lock up the house, and yet she says, "Our house is hell". And then she says to Launcelot Gobbo "Thou . . . didst rob it of some taste of tediousness" as though tediousness was a hellish situation! She behaves appallingly to her father – she elopes, she elopes with a *Christian*, she converts to Christianity, she steals his money and his most sentimental possessions. She's an out-and-out bitch in terms of her relationship to her father. She's certainly on that side a dark character, and yet her love for Lorenzo is total. Every character is a mixture, and that's what we went for mainly in rehearsal – to explore and not hide their various motivations, not pretend they're not there, because I think the richness of the play is in the fact that, like *The News of the World*, all human life is there!'

Leslee Udwin, who played Jessica, has no difficulty with the contradictions in the character. 'I didn't go for a lyrical, romantic young girl in any way. To me she was an immensely passionate and fiery young girl with quite a developed sense of sexuality – in an unexplored way. I feel that she is highly impulsive and so she can embrace all these various facets. Stealing the ducats – I can understand that perfectly. She's hitting back at the thing that has made her life hell – his attitude to those ducats. In a different way I've done the same sort of thing to my own father who's also a very religious Jew. It's as though she's saying, "That was more important than me so now I'll show you!"

'The greatest difficulty is accepting that she exchanged his ring for a monkey, knowing the ring had been her mother's. That hits the hardest of all. Those lines of Shylock's, "It was my turquoise; I had it of Leah when I was a bachelor; I would not have given it for a wilderness of monkeys", for me are some of the most heart-rending in any of Shakespeare's plays. Luckily as an actress I didn't have to think about it too heavily as she is not seen doing it. I never had to come up with a definite answer as to how to do it and I would hate to have had to.

'She only has one scene with Shylock and it's not explicit how he treats her or what degree of hell exists in that house. He says to her, "Clamber not you up to the casements", which gives one an idea of the atmosphere – for a passive, good young girl it might be perfectly OK, but for someone who wants to express all her emotions it's very restrictive, very oppressive. She loves Lorenzo in a very *hot* way – not romantic at all. By becoming a Christian to marry him she has denied her identity in a way but nonetheless that Jewishness is so bound up with her house being hell that when she says "I'll be a Christian" it's an out, that's the way she's going to leave this restrictive atmosphere and give vent to this passion.'

Gemma Jones agrees firmly with Gold that all the characters, including Portia, are a mixture of good and bad. 'One of the joys of the character of Portia is that she's many-faceted,' she says. 'Almost every scene is another of her tones, moods. There are aspects of Portia that shouldn't be whitewashed over. The situation she finds herself in at the beginning of the play – having to follow passively the terms of her father's will in testing her suitors – I hope that we have introduced into it a feeling of extreme frustration with her lot, unable to exert her own will and authority. "I may neither choose who I would nor refuse who I dislike; so is the will of a living daughter curb'd by the will of a dead father." I think when she actually has the law in her own hand she takes centre stage with great force and determination. The way she behaves in the trial scene is very unemotional and strong and punitive and didactic – rather masculine. But the other side is that she has totally succumbed to "love" for Bassanio. If she was in her right mind I think she would know that he's not really at all suitable as a husband, but she's *not* in her right mind: she's in love. I shouldn't think he will make a very good husband! The play does have a sting in the tail.'

'Where we were lucky was in having a Jew play a Jew,' says Gold. In fact, in the gallery there is a degree of jokey Jewish unity: Miller, Gold and Mitchell are all Jewish (though of widely different backgrounds) and they rather enjoy the ironies. 'He's got a Jewish sense of rhythm, that boy,' says Miller approvingly of one of Mitchell's speeches, and offers to put a *mazuzah* on the door leading into the gallery. 'Watching non-Jews trying to be Jews is just awful,' declares Gold. 'I've seen two versions and it's like watching Englishmen trying to be American or Americans trying to be English: it's always phoney. They tack on characteristics that don't make sense; you don't believe it. Since Warren Mitchell is Jewish that problem was solved – there was no way he could act that wasn't Jewish. It was a matter of saying what sort of Jewish is he. There's absolutely no sentimentality or coyness: he's a moneylender from a ghetto in Venice and totally three-dimensionally human, a man who can laugh, suffer, act out of revenge. We're not for a moment setting up the famous speeches as speeches. "Hath not a Jew eyes . . ." – we took the Gettysburg address element out of it very carefully – it springs out of a jew-baiting scene.'

Mitchell gives a performance breathtakingly poised between humour, pathos, revulsion and indignant empathy: 'I'm playing this Jew as a Jew,' he says. 'We had discussions with the director whether I was to use an accent and I wanted to be different from the Christians – I didn't want to be noble, tremendously dignified. I mean, it has been done that way – a proud, dignified man, but I wanted to be a very ordinary human being who at times would say to himself, "Keep cool, I don't want these Christians to see me lose my cool," but nevertheless would lose his cool because he's human, he couldn't help himself.

'I've never suffered any persecution as a Jew; I was never in Germany or anything like that. I tried to imagine myself as a black, how it must have felt say twenty or thirty years ago – although, let's face it, there are plenty of blacks in London now who would identify totally with Shylock! You have to understand why he behaves as a villain – he is attempting murder, no question; he's attempting to kill someone. But if you see the grievances this man has: the play shows them one after another. He's been spat upon and the man who spat on him comes and says, "Listen, Jew, we'd like to borrow 3000 ducats so my friend here can go and chat up some bird in Belmont and put on a great show". I mean, let's face it, Bassanio isn't much more than a gigolo. He's after a rich wife: all right, she's pretty and all that and the love scenes are there and the irony is that it's beautiful poetry in the mouths of people who really . . . they're not very nice. He never, never stops being a villain, but any reasoning person must feel tremendous sympathy for this outcast. The story – it's two stories, the story of Shylock's bond, his revenge, his pound of flesh; and it's the love story of Bassanio and Portia. What hit me constantly as we rehearsed the play is the amazing change that takes place, and it's not unintentional. Those who say that the play is anti-semitic cannot have seen beyond the first level. It was a popular thing at that time to write about Jews in a disparaging way, to make them an object of humour, and if you look at Marlowe's *Jew of Malta* you'll see there a real figure of fun. But Shakespeare wrote this incredible speech, "Hath not a Jew eyes" – but more than that, after this amazing trial scene and the destruction of the Jew – making him become a Christian, taking all his money away from him – Shakespeare then cuts to Belmont, to laughter, to gaiety, to love, to all this fun about the rings. Now that was quite intentional on Shakespeare's part: after this horrific, amazing, terrible destruction of a man, you don't lightly go on . . . no, he was showing a society that was calloused, that didn't care. I would say that no sane person is going to be on the side of Portia – well, yeah! Young lovers! Everyone wants the young lovers to win out, but then you have to analyse what they're about!'

'It is a tremendously difficult end to come to after the trial scene,' Gold acknowledges. 'You end the trial and suddenly the whole play takes off in a different direction. It's like *Twelfth Night* in a lot of ways: I felt a lot of similarities between the way Malvolio is treated and the way Shylock is treated – totally cruel and unfeeling, but that's human life again: they've got rid of Shylock, now they're on to something else. People are like that. And yes, the establishment does get away with it. Establishments do usually, don't they? What's more, they tend to get away with it without any sort of pricked conscience because they assume that's the way it should be.'

It is noticeable, sitting in the gallery through the shooting, how much time Gold spends on the floor – much more, it seems to me, than any other director on the series has previously done. In fact, at one point in the shooting, after rehearsing a scene down in the studio, he declares,' I'm going upstairs for this one.' A cheer breaks out in the gallery upstairs, and then the vision mixer, John Barclay, leans forward to speak into the mike connected to the PA who is down on the floor. 'Tell him we've sold his chair,' he says.

There is a general feeling of good humour, certainly abetted by the fact that Jonathan Miller, the producer, is continually entertaining everyone around him, but mainly springing from the striking warmth of Gold's personality. Tensions arise but they don't survive for long. Everyone jokes with each other. 'Come clean,' says Mitchell to the Antonio, as his chest is bared for the knife, to reveal a sparse arrangement of chest hairs. 'Did the make-up department put those there?' Susan Jameson, as Nerissa, has an entrance and short speech which is accepted in one swift take. 'Makes you wonder, when a *real* artist comes in, doesn't it?' sniffs Warren. 'That's ladies for you,' says Gold consolingly. She proceeds to drop her books in the next take, which delights everyone.

For me one of the oddities of the play has always been the melancholy figure of the merchant himself, Antonio. The fact that the play is named after him even though he is more of a fulcrum than the main subject of any action always gives me pause; yet if one approaches the play trying to give him the importance the title would seem to suggest, the part would appear rather underwritten. Gold, however, disagrees with me: 'I don't think he's underwritten; I think he's very clearly there – it's just a matter of aiming him in the right direction. If you go for it right from the beginning – if you say: what he is about is a man who's in love with Bassanio in whatever area you want to say, and he will do anything to keep Bassanio happy because by keeping him happy he'll keep him in some form or another; and at the same time he's willing to sacrifice himself for Bassanio – if one hits that hard at the beginning, then you understand everything he does right through to the end. In fact, in this production we not only begin the play with Antonio, we end it with him: he's the first person you see and he's the last person you see, and I think it's clear all through what he is. If you don't say that he loves Bassanio, then there is nothing there, because why does he do anything. When they say they love each other you've got to do it in a way that's meant, and not just "Hello, darling". You've got to feel he desperately cares about Bassanio. On the screen the last two people we see are Jessica – a reminder of Shylock – then Antonio. We took him up the steps and then the actor [John Franklyn-Robbins] sat on a bench at the top of the steps, which was a total echo of the beginning of the play. It seemed to me magical and totally unpreconceived – at least by me. I never discussed it with him, before or after. But you could start the play all over again: "In sooth, I *know* why I am so sad," – it's because he loves Bassanio.

'What I did discover working on the play is that there is no one exclusive way of doing Shakespeare. I read an enormous amount about *The Merchant*, lots of different interpretations, and none of them exclude each other. There's no reason why every element from every article can't live with every other approach. There was *no definitive way* of doing it!'

THE BBC TV CAST
AND PRODUCTION TEAM

The cast for the BBC Television production was as follows:

SHYLOCK	Warren Mitchell
PORTIA	Gemma Jones
NERISSA	Susan Jameson
ANTONIO	John Franklyn-Robbins
BASSANIO	John Nettles
GRATIANO	Kenneth Cranham
SALERIO	John Rhys-Davies
SOLANIO	Alan David
LORENZO	Richard Morant
JESSICA	Leslee Udwin
TUBAL	Arnold Diamond
LAUNCELOT GOBBO	Enn Reitel
OLD GOBBO	Joe Gladwin
DUKE OF VENICE	Douglas Wilmer
PRINCE OF MOROCCO	Marc Zuber
PRINCE OF ARRAGON	Peter Gale
LEONARDO	Roger Martin
BALTHASAR	Daniel Mitchell
STEPHANO	Shaun Scott
ANTONIO'S SERVANT	Richard Austin
PRODUCTION ASSISTANT	Tony Garner
DIRECTOR'S ASSISTANT	Beryl Hurdle
PRODUCTION UNIT MANAGER	Fraser Lowden
MUSIC	Carl Davis
LITERARY CONSULTANT	John Wilders
MAKE-UP ARTIST	Marion Richards
COSTUME DESIGNER	Raymond Hughes
SOUND	Chick Anthony
LIGHTING	Dennis Channon
DESIGNER	Oliver Bayldon

SCRIPT EDITOR   David Snodin
PRODUCER   Jonathan Miller
DIRECTOR   Jack Gold

The production was recorded between 15 and 21 May 1980

THE TEXT

The Merchant of Venice was probably written about 1596, and has several possible sources, most notably an Italian story published at the end of the fourteenth century in a collection known as 'Il Pecorone'. The play was first printed in quarto in 1600, then again in a second quarto in 1619, and then again in the 1623 folio, which contained all Shakespeare's completed plays apart from *Pericles*. Further folios were printed in 1632, 1663, 1664 and 1685. The first critical edition of the works appeared in 1709, and was edited by Nicholas Rowe. Rowe was responsible for several stage-directions, and he divided the plays into acts and scenes. There have been countless editions since, with numerous emendations and 'improvements'. The text printed here is from the late Professor Peter Alexander's 1951 edition of the *Complete Works*. This is the text used for all the productions in the BBC Television Shakespeare series.

Under Jonathan Miller's rule as producer of the series, individual directors have been given the freedom to stray from complete textual fidelity on occasion, by cutting, changing or even rearranging the text, if they have felt that their particular approach to a play requires it, and that a viewer's understanding and enjoyment of the play will thereby be enhanced, although we have always tried to bear in the mind the fact that these productions will be seen by millions of people who have never seen a Shakespeare play before, and who should therefore be given the opportunity to experience a version that remains reasonably faithful to the play as it was written. As it happens, Jack Gold, the director of this production of *The Merchant of Venice*, has chosen to be entirely faithful, since he considers the play to be flawlessly structured. Arguably, indeed, it is the most perfectly constructed of all Shakespeare's masterpieces.

As in the other volumes in the BBC Television Shakespeare, the notes in the right-hand margin are designed to be of benefit to those who might wish to compare the text with the television production. Since in this case there have been no cuts, the marginal notes are comparatively few, and simply consist of the odd stage-direction as it appeared in the camera-script prepared for production, including the changes of scene, which are described and numbered as they were in the script. Sometimes a character has been given lines not attributed to him in the printed text, and this is mentioned where it occurs. Occasionally an actor has chosen, in consultation with the director, to change the text slightly, usually in accordance with an edition of the play other than the Alexander, and these small variations are noted. No mention has been made, however, of those rare alterations to the text which are unintentional but nonetheless inevitable in the pressurised and clock-watching atmosphere of a television studio. Every effort was made to avoid such slips, but when a scene can only be recorded three or four times at the most, the version that is finally chosen has to be the best in terms of performance rather than in terms of complete textual accuracy. Neither has reference been made in the margin to the common television practice of 'discovering' characters at the start of a scene, and cutting away before anyone has left, even though the printed text begins each scene with the word 'enter' and concludes it with 'exit' or 'exeunt'.

DAVID SNODIN

THE MERCHANT OF VENICE

DRAMATIS PERSONÆ

THE DUKE OF VENICE.
THE PRINCE OF MOROCCO, } suitors to
THE PRINCE OF ARRAGON } Portia.
ANTONIO, a merchant of Venice.
BASSANIO, his friend, suitor to Portia.
SOLANIO, }
SALERIO, } friends to Antonio
GRATIANO, } and Bassanio.
LORENZO, in love with Jessica.
SHYLOCK, a rich Jew.
TUBAL, a Jew, his friend.
LAUNCELOT GOBBO, a clown, servant
to Shylock.

OLD COBBO, father to Launcelot.
LEONARDO, servant to Bassanio.
BALTHASAR, } servants to Portia.
STEPHANO, }

PORTIA, a rich heiress.
NERISSA, her waiting-maid.
JESSICA, daughter to Shylock.

MAGNIFICOES OF VENICE, OFFICERS
OF THE COURT OF JUSTICE,
GAOLER, SERVANTS, and other
ATTENDANTS.

THE SCENE : Venice, and Portia's house at Belmont.

ACT ONE.

SCENE I. Venice. A street.

Enter ANTONIO, SALERIO, and SOLANIO.

SCENE I
Exterior. Venice.
Day

ANT. In sooth, I know not why I am so sad.
It wearies me ; you say it wearies you ;
But how I caught it, found it, or came by it,
What stuff 'tis made of, whereof it is born,
I am to learn ;
And such a want-wit sadness makes of me
That I have much ado to know myself.
SALER. Your mind is tossing on the ocean ;
There where your argosies, with portly sail—
Like signiors and rich burghers on the flood,
Or as it were the pageants of the sea—
Do overpeer the petty traffickers,
That curtsy to them, do them reverence,
As they fly by them with their woven wings.
SOLAN. Believe me, sir, had I such venture forth,
The better part of my affections would
Be with my hopes abroad. I should be still
Plucking the grass to know where sits the wind,
Peering in maps for ports, and piers, and roads ;
And every object that might make me fear
Misfortune to my ventures, out of doubt,
Would make me sad.
SALER. My wind, cooling my broth,
Would blow me to an ague when I thought

5

10

15

20

What harm a wind too great might do at sea.
I should not see the sandy hour-glass run 25
But I should think of shallows and of flats,
And see my wealthy Andrew dock'd in sand,
Vailing her high top lower than her ribs
To kiss her burial. Should I go to church
And see the holy edifice of stone, 30
And not bethink me straight of dangerous rocks,
Which, touching but my gentle vessel's side,
Would scatter all her spices on the stream,
Enrobe the roaring waters with my silks,
And, in a word, but even now worth this, 35
And now worth nothing ? Shall I have the thought
To think on this, and shall I lack the thought
That such a thing bechanc'd would make me sad ?
But tell not me ; I know Antonio
Is sad to think upon his merchandise. 40
ANT. Believe me, no ; I thank my fortune for it,
My ventures are not in one bottom trusted,
Nor to one place ; nor is my whole estate
Upon the fortune of this present year ;
Therefore my merchandise makes me not sad. 45
SOLAN. Why then you are in love.
ANT. Fie, fie !
SOLAN. Not in love neither ? Then let us say you are sad
Because you are not merry ; and 'twere as easy
For you to laugh and leap and say you are merry,
Because you are not sad. Now, by two-headed Janus, 50
Nature hath fram'd strange fellows in her time :
Some that will evermore peep through their eyes,
And laugh like parrots at a bag-piper ;
And other of such vinegar aspect
That they'll not show their teeth in way of smile 55
Though Nestor swear the jest be laughable.

Enter BASSANIO, LORENZO, *and* GRATIANO.

Here comes Bassanio, your most noble kinsman,
Gratiano and Lorenzo. Fare ye well ;
We leave you now with better company.
SALER. I would have stay'd till I had made you merry, 60
If worthier friends had not prevented me.
ANT. Your worth is very dear in my regard.
I take it your own business calls on you,
And you embrace th' occasion to depart.
SALER. Good morrow, my good lords. 65
BASS. Good signiors both, when shall we laugh ? Say when.
You grow exceeding strange ; must it be so ?
SALER. We'll make our leisures to attend on yours.
[*exeunt* SALERIO *and* SOLANIO.
LOR. My Lord Bassanio, since you have found Antonio,
We two will leave you ; but at dinner-time, 70
I pray you, have in mind where we must meet.
BASS. I will not fail you.
GRA. You look not well, Signior Antonio ;

You have too much respect upon the world ;
They lose it that do buy it with much care.   75
Believe me, you are marvellously chang'd.
ANT. I hold the world but as the world, Gratiano—
A stage, where every man must play a part,
And mine a sad one.
GRA.   Let me play the fool.
With mirth and laughter let old wrinkles come ;   80
And let my liver rather heat with wine
Than my heart cool with mortifying groans.
Why should a man whose blood is warm within
Sit like his grandsire cut in alabaster,
Sleep when he wakes, and creep into the jaundice   85
By being peevish ?   I tell thee what, Antonio—
I love thee, and 'tis my love that speaks—
There are a sort of men whose visages
Do cream and mantle like a standing pond,
And do a wilful stillness entertain,   90
With purpose to be dress'd in an opinion
Of wisdom, gravity, profound conceit ;
As who should say ' I am Sir Oracle,
And when I ope my lips let no dog bark '.
O my Antonio, I do know of these   95
That therefore only are reputed wise
For saying nothing ; when, I am very sure,
If they should speak, would almost damn those ears
Which, hearing them, would call their brothers fools.
I'll tell thee more of this another time.   100
But fish not with this melancholy bait
For this fool gudgeon, this opinion.
Come, good Lorenzo.   Fare ye well awhile ;
I'll end my exhortation after dinner.
LOR. Well, we will leave you then till dinner-time.   105
I must be one of these same dumb wise men,
For Gratiano never lets me speak.
GRA. Well, keep me company but two years moe,
Thou shalt not know the sound of thine own tongue.
ANT. Fare you well ; I'll grow a talker for this gear.   110
GRA. Thanks, i' faith, for silence is only commendable
In a neat's tongue dried, and a maid not vendible.
                          [exeunt GRATIANO and LORENZO.
ANT. Is that anything now ?
BASS. Gratiano speaks an infinite deal of nothing, more than any man
in all Venice.   His reasons are as two grains of wheat hid in two
bushels of chaff : you shall seek all day ere you find them, and
when you have them they are not worth the search.   118
ANT. Well ; tell me now what lady is the same
To whom you swore a secret pilgrimage,
That you to-day promis'd to tell me of ?
BASS. 'Tis not unknown to you, Antonio,
How much I have disabled mine estate
By something showing a more swelling port
Than my faint means would grant continuance ;   125
Nor do I now make moan to be abridg'd

From such a noble rate ; but my chief care
Is to come fairly off from the great debts
Wherein my time, something too prodigal,
Hath left me gag'd.   To you, Antonio,   130
I owe the most, in money and in love ;
And from your love I have a warranty
To unburden all my plots and purposes
How to get clear of all the debts I owe.
ANT. I pray you, good Bassanio, let me know it ;   135
And if it stand, as you yourself still do,
Within the eye of honour, be assur'd
My purse, my person, my extremest means,
Lie all unlock'd to your occasions.
BASS. In my school-days, when I had lost one shaft,   140
I shot his fellow of the self-same flight
The self-same way, with more advised watch,
To find the other forth ; and by adventuring both
I oft found both.   I urge this childhood proof,
Because what follows is pure innocence.   145
I owe you much ; and, like a wilful youth,
That which I owe is lost ; but if you please
To shoot another arrow that self way
Which you did shoot the first, I do not doubt,
As I will watch the aim, or to find both,   150
Or bring your latter hazard back again
And thankfully rest debtor for the first.
ANT. You know me well, and herein spend but time
To wind about my love with circumstance ;
And out of doubt you do me now more wrong   155
In making question of my uttermost
Than if you had made waste of all I have.
Then do but say to me what I should do
That in your knowledge may by me be done,
And I am prest unto it ; therefore, speak.   160
BASS. In Belmont is a lady richly left,
And she is fair and, fairer than that word,
Of wondrous virtues.   Sometimes from her eyes
I did receive fair speechless messages.
Her name is Portia—nothing undervalu'd   165
To Cato's daughter, Brutus' Portia.
Nor is the wide world ignorant of her worth ;
For the four winds blow in from every coast
Renowned suitors, and her sunny locks
Hang on her temples like a golden fleece,   170
Which makes her seat of Belmont Colchos' strond,
And many Jasons come in quest of her.
O my Antonio, had I but the means
To hold a rival place with one of them,
I have a mind presages me such thrift   175
That I should questionless be fortunate.
ANT. Thou know'st that all my fortunes are at sea ;
Neither have I money nor commodity
To raise a present sum ; therefore go forth,
Try what my credit can in Venice do ;   180

That shall be rack'd, even to the uttermost,
To furnish thee to Belmont to fair Portia.
Go presently inquire, and so will I,
Where money is ; and I no question make
To have it of my trust or for my sake.   [*exeunt.*

SCENE II. *Belmont. Portia's house.*

Enter PORTIA *with her waiting-woman,* NERISSA.

SCENE 2
*Exterior. Belmont.
Day.*

POR. By my troth, Nerissa, my little body is aweary of this great
world.
NER. You would be, sweet madam, if your miseries were in the same
abundance as your good fortunes are ; and yet, for aught I see,
they are as sick that surfeit with too much as they that starve with
nothing. It is no mean happiness, therefore, to be seated in the
mean : superfluity comes sooner by white hairs, but competency
lives longer.
POR. Good sentences, and well pronounc'd.
NER. They would be better, if well followed.   10
POR. If to do were as easy as to know what were good to do, chapels
had been churches, and poor men's cottages princes' palaces. It
is a good divine that follows his own instructions ; I can easier
teach twenty what were good to be done than to be one of the
twenty to follow mine own teaching. The brain may devise
laws for the blood, but a hot temper leaps o'er a cold decree ;
such a hare is madness the youth, to skip o'er the meshes of good
counsel the cripple. But this reasoning is not in the fashion to
choose me a husband. O me, the word ' choose ' ! I may
neither choose who I would nor refuse who I dislike ; so is the
will of a living daughter curb'd by the will of a dead father. Is it
not hard, Nerissa, that I cannot choose one, nor refuse none ?23
NER. Your father was ever virtuous, and holy men at their death have
good inspirations ; therefore the lott'ry that he hath devised in
these three chests, of gold, silver, and lead—whereof who chooses
his meaning chooses you—will no doubt never be chosen by any
rightly but one who you shall rightly love. But what warmth is
there in your affection towards any of these princely suitors that
are already come ?   31
POR. I pray thee over-name them ; and as thou namest them, I will
describe them ; and according to my description, level at my
affection.
NER. First, there is the Neapolitan prince.   35
POR. Ay, that's a colt indeed, for he doth nothing but talk of his
horse ; and he makes it a great appropriation to his own good
parts that he can shoe him himself ; I am much afear'd my lady
his mother play'd false with a smith.
NER. Then is there the County Palatine.   40
POR. He doth nothing but frown, as who should say ' An you will not
have me, choose '. He hears merry tales and smiles not. I fear
he will prove the weeping philosopher when he grows old, being so
full of unmannerly sadness in his youth. I had rather be married
to a death's-head with a bone in his mouth than to either of these.
God defend me from these two !

How say you by the French lord, Monsieur Le Bon ?   49
POR. God made him, and therefore let him pass for a man.   In truth,
I know it is a sin to be a mocker, but he—why, he hath a horse
better than the Neapolitan's, a better bad habit of frowning than
the Count Palatine ; he is every man in no man.   If a throstle
sing he falls straight a-cap'ring ; he will fence with his own
shadow ; if I should marry him, I should marry twenty husbands.
If he would despise me, I would forgive him ; for if he love me
to madness, I shall never requite him.
NER. What say you then to Falconbridge, the young baron of
England ?   60
POR. You know I say nothing to him, for he understands not me,
nor I him : he hath neither Latin, French, nor Italian, and you
will come into the court and swear that I have a poor pennyworth
in the English.   He is a proper man's picture ; but alas, who can
converse with a dumb-show ?   How oddly he is suited !   I think
he bought his doublet in Italy, his round hose in France, his
bonnet in Germany, and his behaviour everywhere.   68
NER. What think you of the Scottish lord, his neighbour ?
POR. That he hath a neighbourly charity in him, for he borrowed a
box of the ear of the Englishman, and swore he would pay him
again when he was able ; I think the Frenchman became his
surety, and seal'd under for another.
NER. How like you the young German, the Duke of Saxony's
nephew ?   75
POR. Very vilely in the morning when he is sober ; and most vilely
in the afternoon when he is drunk.   When he is best, he is a little
worse than a man, and when he is worst, he is little better than a
beast.   An the worst fall that ever fell, I hope I shall make shift
to go without him.   80
NER. If he should offer to choose, and choose the right casket, you
should refuse to perform your father's will, if you should refuse
to accept him.
POR. Therefore, for fear of the worst, I pray thee set a deep glass of
Rhenish wine on the contrary casket ; for if the devil be within
and that temptation without, I know he will choose it.   I will do
anything, Nerissa, ere I will be married to a sponge.   88
NER. You need not fear, lady, the having any of these lords ; they
have acquainted me with their determinations, which is indeed
to return to their home, and to trouble you with no more suit, unless you may be won by some other sort than your father's
imposition, depending on the caskets.   94
POR. If I live to be as old as Sibylla, I will die as chaste as Diana,
unless I be obtained by the manner of my father's will.   I am glad
this parcel of wooers are so reasonable ; for there is not one
among them but I dote on his very absence, and I pray God
grant them a fair departure.   99
NER. Do you not remember, lady, in your father's time, a Venetian,
a scholar' and a soldier, that came hither in company of the
Marquis of Montferrat ?
POR. Yes, yes, it was Bassanio ; as I think, so was he call'd.
NER. True, madam ; he, of all the men that ever my foolish eyes
look'd upon, was the best deserving a fair lady.
POR. I remember him well, and I remember him worthy of thy praise.

Enter a SERVINGMAN.

How now ! what news ?　　　　　　　　　　　　　　109
SERV. The four strangers seek for you, madam, to take their leave ;
　and there is a forerunner come from a fifth, the Prince of Morocco,
　who brings word the Prince his master will be here to-night. 113
POR. If I could bid the fifth welcome with so good heart as I can bid
　the other four farewell, I should be glad of his approach ; if he
　have the condition of a saint and the complexion of a devil, I had
　rather he should shrive me than wive me.
Come, Nerissa.　Sirrah, go before.　　　　　　　　118
Whiles we shut the gate upon one wooer, another knocks at the
door.　　　　　　　　　　　　　　　　　　　[*exeunt.*

SCENE III.　*Venice.　A public place.*

Enter BASSANIO *with* SHYLOCK *the* Jew.

SHY. Three thousand ducats—well.
BASS. Ay, sir, for three months.
SHY. For three months—well.
BASS. For the which, as I told you, Antonio shall be bound.
SHY. Antonio shall become bound—well.
BASS. May you stead me ?　Will you pleasure me ?　Shall I know
　your answer ?　　　　　　　　　　　　　　8
SHY. Three thousand ducats for three months, and Antonio bound.
BASS. Your answer to that.
SHY. Antonio is a good man.
BASS. Have you heard any imputation to the contrary ?
SHY. Ho, no, no, no, no ; my meaning in saying he is a good man is
　to have you understand me that he is sufficient ; yet his means
　are in supposition : he hath an argosy bound to Tripolis, another
　to the Indies ; I understand, moreover, upon the Rialto, he hath
　a third at Mexico, a fourth for England—and other ventures he
　hath, squand'red abroad.　But ships are but boards, sailors but
　men ; there be land-rats and water-rats, water-thieves and land-
　thieves—I mean pirates ; and then there is the peril of waters,
　winds, and rocks.　The man is, notwithstanding, sufficient.
　Three thousand ducats—I think I may take his bond.
BASS. Be assur'd you may.　　　　　　　　　　25
SHY. I will be assur'd I may ; and, that I may be assured, I will
　bethink me.　May I speak with Antonio ?
BASS. If it please you to dine with us.
SHY. Yes, to smell pork, to eat of the habitation which your prophet,
　the Nazarite, conjured the devil into !　I will buy with you, sell
　with you, talk with you, walk with you, and so following ; but I
　will not eat with you, drink with you, nor pray with you.　What
　news on the Rialto ?　Who is he comes here ?　　　34

Enter ANTONIO.

BASS. This is Signior Antonio.
SHY. [*aside.*]　How like a fawning publican he looks !
　I hate him for he is a Christian ;
　But more for that in low simplicity
　He lends out money gratis, and brings down

In the television
production the
servingman is
BALTHASAR.

SCENE 3
*Exterior. Venice.
Shylock's Territory.
Day.*

The rate of usance here with us in Venice.   40
If I can catch him once upon the hip,
I will feed fat the ancient grudge I bear him.
He hates our sacred nation ; and he rails,
Even there where merchants most do congregate,
On me, my bargains, and my well-won thrift,   45
Which he calls interest.   Cursed be my tribe
If I forgive him !
BASS.   Shylock, do you hear ?
SHY. I am debating of my present store,
And, by the near guess of my memory,
I cannot instantly raise up the gross   50
Of full three thousand ducats.   What of that ?
Tubal, a wealthy Hebrew of my tribe,
Will furnish me.   But soft ! how many months
Do you desire ? [to Antonio.]   Rest you fair, good signior ;
Your worship was the last man in our mouths.   55
ANT. Shylock, albeit I neither lend nor borrow
By taking nor by giving of excess,
Yet, to supply the ripe wants of my friend,
I'll break a custom. [to Bassanio.]   Is he yet possess'd
How much ye would ?
SHY.   Ay, ay, three thousand ducats.   60
ANT. And for three months.
SHY. I had forgot—three months ; you told me so.
Well then, your bond ; and, let me see—but hear you,
Methoughts you said you neither lend nor borrow
Upon advantage.
ANT.   I do never use it.   65
SHY. When Jacob graz'd his uncle Laban's sheep—
This Jacob from our holy Abram was,
As his wise mother wrought in his behalf,
The third possessor ; ay, he was the third—
ANT. And what of him ?   Did he take interest ?   70
SHY. No, not take interest ; not, as you would say,
Directly int'rest ;   mark what Jacob did :
When Laban and himself were compromis'd
That all the eanlings which were streak'd and pied
Should fall as Jacob's hire, the ewes, being rank,   75
In end of autumn turned to the rams ;
And when the work of generation was
Between these woolly breeders in the act,
The skilful shepherd pill'd me certain wands,
And, in the doing of the deed of kind,   80
He stuck them up before the fulsome ewes,
Who, then conceiving, did in eaning time
Fall parti-colour'd lambs, and those were Jacob's.
This was a way to thrive, and he was blest ;
And thrift is blessing, if men steal it not.   85
ANT. This was a venture, sir, that Jacob serv'd for ;
A thing not in his power to bring to pass,
But sway'd and fashion'd by the hand of heaven.
Was this inserted to make interest good ?
Or is your gold and silver ewes and rams ?   90

SHY. I cannot tell ; I make it breed as fast.
  But note me, signior.
ANT. [aside.]   Mark you this, Bassanio,
  The devil can cite Scripture for his purpose.
  An evil soul producing holy witness
  Is like a villain with a smiling cheek,
  A goodly apple rotten at the heart.   95
  O, what a goodly outside falsehood hath !
SHY. Three thousand ducats—'tis a good round sum.
  Three months from twelve ; then let me see, the rate—
ANT. Well, Shylock, shall we be beholding to you ?   100
SHY. Signior Antonio, many a time and oft
  In the Rialto you have rated me
  About my moneys and my usances ;
  Still have I borne it with a patient shrug,
  For suff'rance is the badge of all our tribe ;   105
  You call me misbeliever, cut-throat dog,
  And spit upon my Jewish gaberdine,
  And all for use of that which is mine own.
  Well then, it now appears you need my help ;
  Go to, then ; you come to me, and you say   110
  ' Shylock, we would have moneys '. You say so—
  You that did void your rheum upon my beard
  And foot me as you spurn a stranger cur
  Over your threshold ; moneys is your suit.
  What should I say to you ? Should I not say   115
  ' Hath a dog money ? Is it possible
  A cur can lend three thousand ducats ? ' Or
  Shall I bend low and, in a bondman's key,
  With bated breath and whisp'ring humbleness,
  Say this :   120
  ' Fair sir, you spit on me on Wednesday last,
  You spurn'd me such a day ; another time
  You call'd me dog ; and for these courtesies
  I'll lend you thus much moneys ' ?
ANT. I am as like to call thee so again,   125
  To spit on thee again, to spurn thee too.
  If thou wilt lend this money, lend it not
  As to thy friends—for when did friendship take
  A breed for barren metal of his friend ?—
  But lend it rather to thine enemy,   130
  Who if he break thou mayst with better face
  Exact the penalty.
SHY. Why, look you, how you storm !
  I would be friends with you, and have your love,
  Forget the shames that you have stain'd me with,
  Supply your present wants, and take no doit   135
  Of usance for my moneys, and you'll not hear me.
  This is kind I offer.
BASS. This were kindness.
SHY.   This kindness will I show.
  Go with me to a notary, seal me there
  Your single bond, and, in a merry sport,   140
  If you repay me not on such a day,

Line 129: 'A breed of
barren metal for his
friend'

39

In such a place, such sum or sums as are
Express'd in the condition, let the forfeit
Be nominated for an equal pound
Of your fair flesh, to be cut off and taken   145
In what part of your body pleaseth me.
ANT. Content, in faith ; I'll seal to such a bond,
And say there is much kindness in the Jew.
BASS. You shall not seal to such a bond for me ;
I'll rather dwell in my necessity.   150
ANT. Why, fear not, man ; I will not forfeit it ;
Within these two months—that's a month before
This bond expires—I do expect return
Of thrice three times the value of this bond.
SHY. O father Abram, what these Christians are,   155
Whose own hard dealings teaches them suspect
The thoughts of others ! Pray you, tell me this :
If he should break his day, what should I gain
By the exaction of the forfeiture ?
A pound of man's flesh taken from a man   160
Is not so estimable, profitable neither,
As flesh of muttons, beefs, or goats. I say,
To buy his favour, I extend this friendship ;
If he will take it, so ; if not, adieu ;
And, for my love, I pray you wrong me not.   165
ANT. Yes, Shylock, I will seal unto this bond.
SHY. Then meet me forthwith at the notary's ;
Give him direction for this merry bond,
And I will go and purse the ducats straight,
See to my house, left in the fearful guard   170
Of an unthrifty knave, and presently
I'll be with you.
ANT.   Hie thee, gentle Jew.
                                        [exit SHYLOCK.
The Hebrew will turn Christian : he grows kind.
BASS. I like not fair terms and a villain's mind.
ANT. Come on ; in this there can be no dismay ;   175
My ships come home a month before the day.   [exeunt.

ACT TWO.

SCENE I. *Belmont. Portia's house.*

Flourish of cornets.   Enter the PRINCE OF MOROCCO, *a tawny Moor all in
white, and three or four* FOLLOWERS *accordingly, with* PORTIA, NERISSA,
and TRAIN.

SCENE 4
*Exterior. Belmont.
Day.*

MOR. Mislike me not for my complexion,
The shadowed livery of the burnish'd sun,
To whom I am a neighbour, and near bred.
Bring me the fairest creature northward born,
Where Phœbus' fire scarce thaws the icicles,   5
And let us make incision for your love
To prove whose blood is reddest, his or mine.
I tell thee, lady, this aspect of mine

The Prince of Morocco (Marc Zuber), Portia (Gemma Jones) and Nerissa (Susan Jameson)

Hath fear'd the valiant ; by my love, I swear
The best-regarded virgins of our clime   10
Have lov'd it too.   I would not change this hue,
Except to steal your thoughts, my gentle queen.
POR. In terms of choice I am not solely led
By nice direction of a maiden's eyes ;
Besides, the lott'ry of my destiny   15
Bars me the right of voluntary choosing.
But, if my father had not scanted me,
And hedg'd me by his wit to yield myself
His wife who wins me by that means I told you,
Yourself, renowned Prince, then stood as fair   20
As any comer I have look'd on yet
For my affection.
MOR.   Even for that I thank you.
Therefore, I pray you, lead me to the caskets
To try my fortune.   By this scimitar,
That slew the Sophy and a Persian prince,   25
That won three fields of Sultan Solyman,
I would o'erstare the sternest eyes that look,
Outbrave the heart most daring on the earth,
Pluck the young sucking cubs from the she-bear,
Yea, mock the lion when 'a roars for prey,   30
To win thee, lady.   But, alas the while !
If Hercules and Lichas play at dice
Which is the better man, the greater throw
May turn by fortune from the weaker hand.
So is Alcides beaten by his page ;   35
And so may I, blind Fortune leading me,
Miss that which one unworthier may attain,
And die with grieving.
POR.   You must take your chance,
And either not attempt to choose at all,
Or swear before you choose, if you choose wrong,   40
Never to speak to lady afterward
In way of marriage ; therefore be advis'd.
MOR. Nor will not ; come, bring me unto my chance.
POR. First, forward to the temple.   After dinner
Your hazard shall be made.
MOR.   Good fortune then,   45
To make me blest or cursed'st among men !   [cornets, and exeunt.

SCENE II.   Venice.   A street.

Enter LAUNCELOT GOBBO.

LAUN. Certainly my conscience will serve me to run from this Jew
my master.   The fiend is at mine elbow and tempts me, saying
to me ' Gobbo, Launcelot Gobbo, good Launcelot ' or ' good
Gobbo ' or ' good Launcelot Gobbo, use your legs, take the start,
run away '.   My conscience says ' No ;   take heed, honest
Launcelot, take heed, honest Gobbo ' or, as aforesaid, ' honest
Launcelot Gobbo, do not run ;   scorn running with thy heels '.
Well, the most courageous fiend bids me pack.   ' Via ! ' says the
fiend ;   ' away ! ' says the fiend.   ' For the heavens, rouse up a
brave mind ' says the fiend ' and run.'   Well, my conscience,

SCENE 5
Exterior. Venice.
Canal. Day.

hanging about the neck of my heart, says very wisely to me ' My
honest friend Launcelot, being an honest man's son ' or rather
' an honest woman's son ' ; for indeed my father did something
smack, something grow to, he had a kind of taste—well, my
conscience says ' Launcelot, budge not '. ' Budge ' says the fiend.
' Budge not ' says my conscience. ' Conscience,' say I ' you
counsel well.' ' Fiend,' say I ' you counsel well.' To be rul'd
by my conscience, I should stay with the Jew my master, who—
God bless the mark !—is a kind of devil ; and, to run away from
the Jew, I should be ruled by the fiend, who—saving your
reverence !—is the devil himself. Certainly the Jew is the very
devil incarnation ; and, in my conscience, my conscience is but a
kind of hard conscience to offer to counsel me to stay with the Jew.
The fiend gives the more friendly counsel. I will run, fiend ;
my heels are at your commandment ; I will run.   27

Enter OLD GOBBO, *with a basket.*

GOB. Master young man, you, I pray you, which is the way to master
   Jew's ?
LAUN. [*aside.*] O heavens ! This is my true-begotten father, who,
   being more than sand-blind, high-gravel blind, knows me not.
   I will try confusions with him.
GOB. Master young gentleman, I pray you, which is the way to
   master Jew's ?   34
LAUN. Turn up on your right hand at the next turning, but, at the
   next turning of all, on your left ; marry, at the very next turning,
   turn of no hand, but turn down indirectly to the Jew's house.
GOB. Be God's sonties, 'twill be a hard way to hit ! Can you tell me
   whether one Launcelot, that dwells with him, dwell with him
   or no ?   41
LAUN. Talk you of young Master Launcelot ? [*aside.*] Mark me now ;
   now will I raise the waters.—Talk you of young Master Launcelot ?
GOB. No master, sir, but a poor man's son ; his father, though I say't,
   is an honest exceeding poor man, and, God be thanked, well to live.
LAUN. Well, let his father be what 'a will, we talk of young Master
   Launcelot.
GOB. Your worship's friend, and Launcelot, sir.   50
LAUN. But I pray you, ergo, old man, ergo, I beseech you, talk you of
   young Master Launcelot ?
GOB. Of Launcelot, an't please your mastership.
LAUN. Ergo, Master Launcelot. Talk not of Master Launcelot,
   father ; for the young gentleman, according to Fates and Destinies
   and such odd sayings, the Sisters Three and such branches of
   learning, is indeed deceased ; or, as you would say in plain terms,
   gone to heaven.
GOB. Marry, God forbid ! The boy was the very staff of my age,
   my very prop.   60
LAUN. Do I look like a cudgel or a hovel-post, a staff or a prop ? Do
   you know me, father ?
GOB. Alack the day, I know you not, young gentleman ; but I pray
   you tell me, is my boy—God rest his soul !—alive or dead ?
LAUN. Do you not know me, father ?
GOB. Alack, sir, I am sand-blind ; I know you not.   67
LAUN. Nay, indeed, if you had your eyes, you might fail of the knowing

me : it is a wise father that knows his own child. Well, old man, I will tell you news of your son. Give me your blessing ; truth will come to light ; murder cannot be hid long ; a man's son may, but in the end truth will out.

GOB. Pray you, sir, stand up ; I am sure you are not Launcelot my boy.

LAUN. Pray you, let's have no more fooling about it, but give me your blessing ; I am Launcelot, your boy that was, your son that is, your child that shall be. 78

GOB. I cannot think you are my son.

LAUN. I know not what I shall think of that ; but I am Launcelot, the Jew's man, and I am sure Margery your wife is my mother.

GOB. Her name is Margery, indeed. I'll be sworn, if thou be Launcelot, thou art mine own flesh and blood. Lord worshipp'd might he be, what a beard hast thou got ! Thou hast got more hair on thy chin than Dobbin my fill-horse has on his tail. 87

LAUN. It should seem, then, that Dobbin's tail grows backward ; I am sure he had more hair of his tail than I have of my face when I last saw him.

GOB. Lord, how art thou chang'd ! How dost thou and thy master agree ? I have brought him a present. How 'gree you now ?

LAUN. Well, well ; but, for mine own part, as I have set up my rest to run away, so I will not rest till I have run some ground. My master's a very Jew. Give him a present ! Give him a halter. I am famish'd in his service ; you may tell every finger I have with my ribs. Father, I am glad you are come ; give me your present to one Master Bassanio, who indeed gives rare new liveries ; if I serve not him, I will run as far as God has any ground. O rare fortune ! Here comes the man. To him, father, for I am a Jew, if I serve the Jew any longer. 103

Enter BASSANIO, *with* LEONARDO, *with a* FOLLOWER *or two.*

BASS. You may do so ; but let it be so hasted that supper be ready at the farthest by five of the clock. See these letters delivered, put the liveries to making, and desire Gratiano to come anon to my lodging. [*exit a servant.*

LAUN. To him, father.

GOB. God bless your worship !

BASS. Gramercy ; wouldst thou aught with me ? 110

GOB. Here's my son, sir, a poor boy—

LAUN. Not a poor boy, sir, but the rich Jew's man, that would, sir, as my father shall specify—

GOB. He hath a great infection, sir, as one would say, to serve— 115

LAUN. Indeed the short and the long is, I serve the Jew, and have a desire, as my father shall specify—

GOB. His master and he, saving your worship's reverence, are scarce cater-cousins— 119

LAUN. To be brief, the very truth is that the Jew, having done me wrong, doth cause me, as my father, being I hope an old man, shall frutify unto you—

GOB. I have here a dish of doves that I would bestow upon your worship ; and my suit is— 124

LAUN. In very brief, the suit is impertinent to myself, as your worship shall know by this honest old man ; and, though I say it, though old man, yet poor man, my father.

BASS. One speak for both. What would you ?

LAUN. Serve you sir.
GOB. That is the very defect of the matter, sir.   130
BASS. I know thee well; thou hast obtain'd thy suit.
Shylock thy master spoke with me this day,
And hath preferr'd thee, if it be preferment
To leave a rich Jew's service to become
The follower of so poor a gentleman.   135
LAUN. The old proverb is very well parted between my master
Shylock and you, sir: you have the grace of God, sir, and he
hath enough.
BASS. Thou speak'st it well. Go, father, with thy son.
Take leave of thy old master, and inquire   140
My lodging out. [to a servant.] Give him a livery
More guarded than his fellows'; see it done.
LAUN. Father, in. I cannot get a service, no! I have ne'er a tongue
in my head! [looking on his palm.] Well; if any man in Italy
have a fairer table which doth offer to swear upon a book—I shall
have good fortune. Go to, here's a simple line of life; here's
a small trifle of wives; alas, fifteen wives is nothing; a'leven
widows and nine maids is a simple coming-in for one man. And
then to scape drowning thrice, and to be in peril of my life with
the edge of a feather-bed—here are simple scapes. Well, if
Fortune be a woman, she's a good wench for this gear. Father,
come; I'll take my leave of the Jew in the twinkling.   153
                        [exeunt LAUNCELOT and OLD GOBBO.
BASS. I pray thee, good Leonardo, think on this.
These things being bought and orderly bestowed,   155
Return in haste, for I do feast to-night
My best esteem'd acquaintance; hie thee, go.
LEON. My best endeavours shall be done herein.

                        Enter GRATIANO.

GRA. Where's your master?
LEON.   Yonder, sir, he walks.   [*exit.*
GRA. Signior Bassanio!   160
BASS. Gratiano!
GRA. I have suit to you.
BASS.   You have obtain'd it.
GRA. You must not deny me: I must go with you to Belmont.
BASS. Why, then you must. But hear thee, Gratiano: 165
Thou art too wild, too rude, and bold of voice—
Parts that become thee happily enough,
And in such eyes as ours appear not faults;
But where thou art not known, why there they show
Something too liberal. Pray thee, take pain   170
To allay with some cold drops of modesty
Thy skipping spirit; lest through thy wild behaviour
I be misconst'red in the place I go to
And lose my hopes.
GRA.   Signior Bassanio, hear me:
If I do not put on a sober habit,   175
Talk with respect, and swear but now and then,
Wear prayer-books in my pocket, look demurely,
Nay more, while grace is saying hood mine eyes

Thus with my hat, and sigh, and say amen,
Use all the observance of civility   180
Like one well studied in a sad ostent
To please his grandam, never trust me more.
BASS. Well, we shall see your bearing.
GRA. Nay, but I bar to-night ; you shall not gauge me
By what we do to-night.
BASS.   No, that were pity ;   185
I would entreat you rather to put on
Your boldest suit of mirth, for we have friends
That purpose merriment.   But fare you well ;
I have some business.
GRA. And I must to Lorenzo and the rest ;   190
But we will visit you at supper-time.   [*exeunt.*

SCENE III.   *Venice.   Shylock's house.*

Enter JESSICA *and* LAUNCELOT.

SCENE 6
*Interior. Venice.
Shylock's House.
Day*

JES. I am sorry thou wilt leave my father so.
Our house is hell ; and thou, a merry devil,
Didst rob it of some taste of tediousness.
But fare thee well ; there is a ducat for thee ;
And, Launcelot, soon at supper shalt thou see   5
Lorenzo, who is thy new master's guest.
Give him this letter ; do it secretly.
And so farewell.   I would not have my father
See me in talk with thee.   9
LAUN. Adieu ! tears exhibit my tongue.   Most beautiful pagan,
most sweet Jew !   If a Christian do not play the knave and get
thee, I am much deceived.   But, adieu ! these foolish drops do
something drown my manly spirit ; adieu !
JES. Farewell, good Launcelot.   [*exit.*
Alack, what heinous sin is it in me
To be asham'd to be my father's child !
But though I am a daughter to his blood,
I am not to his manners.   O Lorenzo,
If thou keep promise, I shall end this strife,   20
Become a Christian and thy loving wife.   [*exit.*

SCENE IV.   *Venice.   A street.*

Enter GRATIANO, LORENZO, SALERIO, *and* SOLANIO.

SCENE 7
*Exterior. Venice.
Day.*

LOR. Nay, we will slink away in suppertime,
Disguise us at my lodging, and return
All in an hour.
GRA. We have not made good preparation.
SALER. We have not spoke us yet of torch-bearers.   5
SOLAN. 'Tis vile, unless it may be quaintly ordered ;
And better in my mind not undertook.
LOR. 'Tis now but four o'clock ; we have two hours
To furnish us.

Enter LAUNCELOT, *with a letter.*

Friend Launcelot, what's the news ?   10

LAUN. An it shall please you to break up this, it shall seem to signify.
LOR. I know the hand ; in faith, 'tis a fair hand,
  And whiter than the paper it writ on
  Is the fair hand that writ.
GRA.   Love-news, in faith !
LAUN. By your leave, sir.   15
LOR. Whither goest thou ?
LAUN. Marry, sir, to bid my old master, the Jew, to sup to-night
  with my new master, the Christian.
LOR. Hold, here, take this. Tell gentle Jessica
  I will not fail her ; speak it privately.   20
  Go, gentlemen,   [exit LAUNCELOT.
  Will you prepare you for this masque to-night ?
  I am provided of a torch-bearer.
SALER. Ay, marry, I'll be gone about it straight.
SOLAN. And so will I.
LOR.   Meet me and Gratiano   25
  At Gratiano's lodging some hour hence.
SALER. 'Tis good we do so.
                              [exeunt SALERIO and SOLANIO.
GRA. Was not that letter from fair Jessica ?
LOR. I must needs tell thee all. She hath directed
  How I shall take her from her father's house ;   30
  What gold and jewels she is furnish'd with ;
  What page's suit she hath in readiness.
  If e'er the Jew her father come to heaven,
  It will be for his gentle daughter's sake ;
  And never dare misfortune cross her foot,   35
  Unless she do it under this excuse,
  That she is issue to a faithless Jew.
  Come, go with me, peruse this as thou goest ;
  Fair Jessica shall be my torch-bearer.   [exeunt.

              SCENE V. Venice. Before Shylock's house.   SCENE 8
                                                                   Exterior. Venice.
                   Enter SHYLOCK and LAUNCELOT.   Shylock's Territory.
                                                                   Day.
SHY. Well, thou shalt see ; thy eyes shall be thy judge,
  The difference of old Shylock and Bassanio—
  What, Jessica !—Thou shalt not gormandize
  As thou hast done with me—What, Jessica !—
  And sleep and snore, and rend apparel out—   5
  Why, Jessica, I say !
LAUN.   Why, Jessica !
SHY. Who bids thee call ? I do not bid thee call.
LAUN. Your worship was wont to tell me I could do nothing without
  bidding.

                        Enter JESSICA.

JES. Call you ? What is your will ?   10
SHY. I am bid forth to supper, Jessica ;
  There are my keys. But wherefore should I go ?
  I am not bid for love ; they flatter me ;
  But yet I'll go in hate, to feed upon
  The prodigal Christian. Jessica, my girl,   15

                              47

Enn Reitel as Launcelot Gobbo and Leslee Udwin as Jessica

Look to my house. I am right loath to go ;
There is some ill a-brewing towards my rest,
For I did dream of money-bags to-night.
LAUN. I beseech you, sir, go ; my young master doth expect your
  reproach.   20
SHY. So do I his.
LAUN. And they have conspired together ; I will not say you shall
  see a masque, but if you do, then it was not for nothing that my
  nose fell a-bleeding on Black Monday last at six o'clock i' th'
  morning, falling out that year on Ash Wednesday was four year,
  in th' afternoon.   26
SHY. What, are there masques ? Hear you me, Jessica :
  Lock up my doors, and when you hear the drum,
  And the vile squealing of the wry-neck'd fife,
  Clamber not you up to the casements then,   30
  Nor thrust your head into the public street
  To gaze on Christian fools with varnish'd faces ;
  But stop my house's ears—I mean my casements ;
  Let not the sound of shallow fopp'ry enter
  My sober house. By Jacob's staff, I swear   35
  I have no mind of feasting forth to-night ;
  But I will go. Go you before me, sirrah ;
  Say I will come.
LAUN. I will go before, sir. Mistress, look out at window for all this.
  There will come a Christian by
  Will be worth a Jewess' eye.   [exit.
SHY. What says that fool of Hagar's offspring, ha ?
JES. His words were ' Farewell, mistress' ; nothing else.
SHY. The patch is kind enough, but a huge feeder,   45
  Snail-slow in profit, and he sleeps by day
  More than the wild-cat ; drones hive not with me,
  Therefore I part with him ; and part with him
  To one that I would have him help to waste
  His borrowed purse. Well, Jessica, go in ;   50
  Perhaps I will return immediately.
  Do as I bid you, shut doors after you.
  Fast bind, fast find—
  A proverb never stale in thrifty mind.   [exit.
JES. Farewell ; and if my fortune be not crost,   55
  I have a father, you a daughter, lost.   [exit.

SCENE VI. Venice. Before Shylock's house.

Enter the maskers, GRATIANO and SALERIO.

GRA. This is the pent-house under which Lorenzo
  Desired us to make stand.
SALER.   His hour is almost past.
GRA. And it is marvel he out-dwells his hour,
  For lovers ever run before the clock.
SALER. O, ten times faster Venus' pigeons fly   5
  To seal love's bonds new made than they are wont
  To keep obliged faith unforfeited !
GRA. That ever holds : who riseth from a feast
  With that keen appetite that he sits down ?

SCENE 9
Exterior. Venice.
Shylock's Territory.
Night.
SOLANIO is among the
maskers.

Kenneth Cranham as Gratiano, Richard Morant as Lorenzo and John Rhys-Davies as Salerio

Where is the horse that doth untread again   10
His tedious measures with the unbated fire
That he did pace them first ?   All things that are
Are with more spirit chased than enjoyed.
How like a younker or a prodigal
The scarfed bark puts from her native bay,   15
Hugg'd and embraced by the strumpet wind ;
How like the prodigal doth she return,
With over-weather'd ribs and ragged sails,
Lean, rent, and beggar'd by the strumpet wind !

Enter LORENZO.

SALER. Here comes Lorenzo ; more of this hereafter.   20
LOR. Sweet friends, your patience for my long abode !
Not I, but my affairs, have made you wait.
When you shall please to play the thieves for wives,
I'll watch as long for you then.   Approach ;
Here dwells my father Jew.   Ho ! who's within ?   25

Enter JESSICA, *above, in boy's clothes.*

JES. Who are you ?   Tell me, for more certainty,
Albeit I'll swear that I do know your tongue.
LOR. Lorenzo, and thy love.
JES. Lorenzo, certain ; and my love indeed ;
For who love I so much ?   And now who knows   30
But you, Lorenzo, whether I am yours ?
LOR. Heaven and thy thoughts are witness that thou art.
JES. Here, catch this casket ; it is worth the pains.
I am glad 'tis night, you do not look on me,
For I am much asham'd of my exchange ;   35
But love is blind, and lovers cannot see
The pretty follies that themselves commit,
For, if they could, Cupid himself would blush
To see me thus transformed to a boy.
LOR. Descend, for you must be my torch-bearer.   40
JES. What ! must I hold a candle to my shames ?
They in themselves, good sooth, are too too light.
Why, 'tis an office of discovery, love,
And I should be obscur'd.
LOR.   So are you, sweet,
Even in the lovely garnish of a boy.   45
But come at once,
For the close night doth play the runaway,
And we are stay'd for at Bassanio's feast.
JES. I will make fast the doors, and gild myself
With some moe ducats, and be with you straight.   [*exit above.*
GRA. Now, by my hood, a gentle, and no Jew.
LOR. Beshrew me, but I love her heartily,
For she is wise, if I can judge of her,
And fair she is, if that mine eyes be true,
And true she is, as she hath prov'd herself ;   55
And therefore, like herself, wise, fair, and true,
Shall she be placed in my constant soul.

Enter JESSICA, *below.*

What, art thou come ?   On, gentlemen, away ;
Our masquing mates by this time for us stay.
        [exit with JESSICA *and* SALERIO.   SOLANIO leaves with
       Enter ANTONIO.   them.
ANT. Who's there ?   60
GRA. Signior Antonio ?
ANT. Fie, fie, Gratiano, where are all the rest ?
  'Tis nine o'clock ; our friends all stay for you ;
  No masque to-night ; the wind is come about ;
  Bassanio presently will go aboard ;   65
  I have sent twenty out to seek for you.
GRA. I am glad on't ; I desire no more delight
  Than to be under sail and gone to-night.   *[exeunt.*

      SCENE VII. *Belmont. Portia's house.*   SCENE 10
           Exterior. Belmont.
Flourish of Cornets. Enter PORTIA, *with the* PRINCE OF MOROCCO, *Night.*
          and their TRAINS.

POR. Go draw aside the curtains and discover
  The several caskets to this noble Prince.
  Now make your choice.
MOR. The first, of gold, who this inscription bears :
  ' Who chooseth me shall gain what many men desire '.   5
  The second, silver, which this promise carries :
  ' Who chooseth me shall get as much as he deserves '.
  This third, dull lead, with warning all as blunt :
  ' Who chooseth me must give and hazard all he hath '.
  How shall I know if I do choose the right ?   10
POR. The one of them contains my picture, Prince ;
  If you choose that, then I am yours withal.
MOR. Some god direct my judgment ! Let me see ;
  I will survey th' inscriptions back again.
  What says this leaden casket ?   15
  ' Who chooseth me must give and hazard all he hath.'
  Must give—for what ?   For lead ?   Hazard for lead !
  This casket threatens ; men that hazard all
  Do it in hope of fair advantages.
  A golden mind stoops not to shows of dross ;   20
  I'll then nor give nor hazard aught for lead.
  What says the silver with her virgin hue ?
  ' Who chooseth me shall get as much as he deserves.'
  As much as he deserves ! Pause there, Morocco,
  And weigh thy value with an even hand.   25
  If thou beest rated by thy estimation,
  Thou dost deserve enough, and yet enough
  May not extend so far as to the lady ;
  And yet to be afeard of my deserving
  Were but a weak disabling of myself.   30
  As much as I deserve ?   Why, that's the lady !
  I do in birth deserve her, and in fortunes,
  In graces, and in qualities of breeding ;
  But more than these, in love I do deserve.
  What if I stray'd no farther, but chose here ?   35
  Let's see once more this saying grav'd in gold :

'Who chooseth me shall gain what many men desire'.
Why, that's the lady! All the world desires her;
From the four corners of the earth they come
To kiss this shrine, this mortal-breathing saint.   40
The Hyrcanian deserts and the vasty wilds
Of wide Arabia are as throughfares now
For princes to come view fair Portia.
The watery kingdom, whose ambitious head
Spits in the face of heaven, is no bar   45
To stop the foreign spirits, but they come
As o'er a brook to see fair Portia.
One of these three contains her heavenly picture.
Is't like that lead contains her? 'Twere damnation
To think so base a thought; it were too gross   50
To rib her cerecloth in the obscure grave.
Or shall I think in silver she's immur'd,
Being ten times undervalued to tried gold?
O sinful thought! Never so rich a gem
Was set in worse than gold. They have in England   55
A coin that bears the figure of an angel
Stamp'd in gold; but that's insculp'd upon.
But here an angel in a golden bed
Lies all within. Deliver me the key;
Here do I choose, and thrive I as I may!   60
POR. There, take it, Prince, and if my form lie there,
Then I am yours.   [*he opens the golden casket.*
MOR.   O hell! what have we here?
A carrion Death, within whose empty eye
There is a written scroll! I'll read the writing.
'All that glisters is not gold,   65
Often have you heard that told;
Many a man his life hath sold
But my outside to behold.
Gilded tombs do worms infold.
Had you been as wise as bold,   70
Young in limbs, in judgment old,
Your answer had not been inscroll'd.
Fare you well, your suit is cold.'

Cold indeed, and labour lost,
Then farewell, heat, and welcome, frost.   75
Portia, adieu! I have too griev'd a heart
To take a tedious leave; thus losers part.
                    [*exit with his train. Flourish of cornets.*
POR. A gentle riddance. Draw the curtains, go.
Let all of his complexion choose me so.   [*exeunt.*

SCENE VIII. *Venice. A street.*   SCENE 11
                                           Exterior. Venice.
Enter SALERIO *and* SOLANIO.   *Day.*

SALER. Why, man, I saw Bassanio under sail;
With him is Gratiano gone along;
And in their ship I am sure Lorenzo is not.
SOLAN. The villain Jew with outcries rais'd the Duke,

53

Who went with him to search Bassanio's ship.   5
SALER. He came too late, the ship was under sail ;
But there the Duke was given to understand
That in a gondola were seen together
Lorenzo and his amorous Jessica ;
Besides, Antonio certified the Duke   10
They were not with Bassanio in his ship.
SOLAN. I never heard a passion so confus'd,
So strange, outrageous, and so variable,
As the dog Jew did utter in the streets.
' My daughter ! O my ducats ! O my daughter !   15
Fled with a Christian ! O my Christian ducats !
Justice ! the law ! My ducats and my daughter !
A sealed bag, two sealed bags of ducats,
Of double ducats, stol'n from me by my daughter !
And jewels—two stones, two rich and precious stones,   20
Stol'n by my daughter ! Justice ! Find the girl ;
She hath the stones upon her and the ducats.'
SALER. Why all the boys in Venice follow him,
Crying, his stones, his daughter, and his ducats.
SOLAN. Let good Antonio look he keep his day,   25
Or he shall pay for this.
SALER.   Marry, well rememb'red ,
I reason'd with a Frenchman yesterday,
Who told me, in the narrow seas that part
The French and English, there miscarried
A vessel of our country richly fraught.   30
I thought upon Antonio when he told me,
And wish'd in silence that it were not his.
SOLAN. You were best to tell Antonio what you hear ;
Yet do not suddenly, for it may grieve him.
SALER. A kinder gentleman treads not the earth.   35
I saw Bassanio and Antonio part.
Bassanio told him he would make some speed
Of his return. He answered ' Do not so ;
Slubber not business for my sake, Bassanio,
But stay the very riping of the time ;   40
And for the Jew's bond which he hath of me,
Let it not enter in your mind of love ;
Be merry, and employ your chiefest thoughts
To courtship, and such fair ostents of love
As shall conveniently become you there '.   45
And even there, his eye being big with tears,
Turning his face, he put his hand behind him,
And with affection wondrous sensible
He wrung Bassanio's hand ; and so they parted.
SOLAN. I think he only loves the world for him.   50
I pray thee, let us go and find him out,
And quicken his embraced heaviness
With some delight or other.
SALER.   Do we so.   [exeunt.

SCENE IX. *Belmont. Portia's house.*

Enter NERISSA, *and a* SERVITOR.

NER. Quick, quick, I pray thee, draw the curtain straight;
The Prince of Arragon hath ta'en his oath,
And comes to his election presently.

Flourish of Cornets. *Enter the* PRINCE OF ARRAGON, PORTIA, *and their*
TRAINS.

POR. Behold, there stand the caskets, noble Prince.
If you choose that wherein I am contain'd,   5
Straight shall our nuptial rites be solemniz'd;
But if you fail, without more speech, my lord,
You must be gone from hence immediately.
AR. I am enjoin'd by oath to observe three things:
First, never to unfold to any one   10
Which casket 'twas I chose; next, if I fail
Of the right casket, never in my life
To woo a maid in way of marriage;
Lastly,
If I do fail in fortune of my choice,   15
Immediately to leave you and be gone.
POR. To these injunctions every one doth swear
That comes to hazard for my worthless self.
AR. And so have I address'd me. Fortune now
To my heart's hope! Gold, silver, and base lead.   20
'Who chooseth me must give and hazard all he hath.'
You shall look fairer ere I give or hazard.
What says the golden chest? Ha! let me see:
'Who chooseth me shall gain what many men desire.'
What many men desire—that 'many' may be meant   25
By the fool multitude, that choose by show,
Not learning more than the fond eye doth teach;
Which pries not to th' interior, but, like the martlet,
Builds in the weather on the outward wall,
Even in the force and road of casualty.   30
I will not choose what many men desire,
Because I will not jump with common spirits
And rank me with the barbarous multitudes.
Why, then to thee, thou silver treasure-house!
Tell me once more what title thou dost bear.   35
'Who chooseth me shall get as much as he deserves.'
And well said too; for who shall go about
To cozen fortune, and be honourable
Without the stamp of merit? Let none presume
To wear an undeserved dignity.   40
O that estates, degrees, and offices,
Were not deriv'd corruptly, and that clear honour
Were purchas'd by the merit of the wearer!
How many then should cover that stand bare!
How many be commanded that command!   45
How much low peasantry would then be gleaned
From the true seed of honour! and how much honour
Pick'd from the chaff and ruin of the times,

SCENE 12
*Exterior. Belmont.
Day.*
The Servitor is
BALTHASAR.

The curtains are
drawn aside to reveal
the waiting
characters.

To be new varnish'd ! Well, but to my choice.
'Who chooseth me shall get as much as he deserves.'   50
I will assume desert. Give me a key for this,
And instantly unlock my fortunes here.
                              [*he opens the silver casket.*
POR. [*aside.*] Too long a pause for that which you find there.
AR. What's here ? The portrait of a blinking idiot
Presenting me a schedule ! I will read it.   55
How much unlike art thou to Portia !
How much unlike my hopes and my deservings !
'Who chooseth me shall have as much as he deserves.'
Did I deserve no more than a fool's head ?
Is that my prize ? Are my deserts no better ?   60
POR. To offend and judge are distinct offices
And of opposed natures.
AR.   What is here ?   [*reads.*
        'The fire seven times tried this ;
        Seven times tried that judgment is
        That did never choose amiss.   65
        Some there be that shadows kiss,
        Such have but a shadow's bliss.
        There be fools alive iwis
        Silver'd o'er, and so was this.
        Take what wife you will to bed,   70
        I will ever be your head.
        So be gone ; you are sped.'

        Still more fool I shall appear
        By the time I linger here.
        With one fool's head I came to woo,   75
        But I go away with two.
        Sweet, adieu ! I'll keep my oath,
        Patiently to bear my wroth.   [*exit with his Train.*
POR. Thus hath the candle sing'd the moth.
O, these deliberate fools ! When they do choose,   80
They have the wisdom by their wit to lose.
NER. The ancient saying is no heresy :
Hanging and wiving goes by destiny.
POR. Come, draw the curtain, Nerissa.

                  Enter a SERVANT.   *Enter* BALTHASAR.

SERV. Where is my lady ?   BALTHASAR.
POR.   Here ; what would my lord ?   85
SERV. Madam, there is alighted at your gate   BALTHASAR.
A young Venetian, one that comes before
To signify th' approaching of his lord,
From whom he bringeth sensible regreets ;
To wit, besides commends and courteous breath,   90
Gifts of rich value. Yet I have not seen
So likely an ambassador of love.
A day in April never came so sweet
To show how costly summer was at hand
As this fore-spurrer comes before his lord.   95
POR. No more, I pray thee ; I am half afeard

Thou wilt say anon he is some kin to thee,
Thou spend'st such high-day wit in praising him.
Come, come, Nerissa, for I long to see
Quick Cupid's post that comes so mannerly.   100
NER. Bassanio, Lord Love, if thy will it be !   [exeunt.

ACT THREE.   SCENE 13
                                                 Exterior. Venice.
SCENE I. Venice. A street.   Day

Enter SOLANIO and SALERIO.

SOLAN. Now, what news on the Rialto ?
SALER. Why, yet it lives there uncheck'd that Antonio hath a ship of
rich lading wreck'd on the narrow seas ; the Goodwins I think
they call the place, a very dangerous flat and fatal, where the
carcases of many a tall ship lie buried, as they say, if my gossip
Report be an honest woman of her word.   7
SOLAN. I would she were as lying a gossip in that as ever knapp'd
ginger or made her neighbours believe she wept for the death
of a third husband. But it is true, without any slips of prolixity
or crossing the plain highway of talk, that the good Antonio, the
honest Antonio——O that I had a title good enough to keep his
name company !—   13
SALER. Come, the full stop.
SOLAN. Ha ! What sayest thou ? Why, the end is, he hath lost a
ship.
SALER. I would it might prove the end of his losses.
SOLAN. Let me say amen betimes, lest the devil cross my prayer, for
here he comes in the likeness of a Jew.

Enter SHYLOCK.

How now, Shylock ? What news among the merchants ?   20
SHY. You knew, none so well, none so well as you, of my daughter's
flight.
SALER. That's certain ; I, for my part, knew the tailor that made the
wings she flew withal.
SOLAN. And Shylock, for his own part, knew the bird was fledge ;
and then it is the complexion of them all to leave the dam.
SHY. She is damn'd for it.
SALER. That's certain, if the devil may be her judge.
SHY. My own flesh and blood to rebel !   30
SOLAN. Out upon it, old carrion ! Rebels it at these years ?
SHY. I say my daughter is my flesh and my blood.
SALER. There is more difference between thy flesh and hers than
between jet and ivory ; more between your bloods than there is
between red wine and Rhenish. But tell us, do you hear whether
Antonio have had any loss at sea or no ?   36
SHY. There I have another bad match : a bankrupt, a prodigal, who
dare scarce show his head on the Rialto ; a beggar, that was us'd
to come so smug upon the mart. Let him look to his bond. He
was wont to call me usurer ; let him look to his bond. He was
wont to lend money for a Christian courtesy ; let him look to his
bond.   42

Arnold Diamond as Tubal and Warren Mitchell as Shylock

SALER. Why, I am sure, if he forfeit, thou wilt not take his flesh.
What's that good for ?   44
SHY. To bait fish withal. If it will feed nothing else, it will feed my
revenge. He hath disgrac'd me and hind'red me half a million;
laugh'd at my losses, mock'd at my gains, scorned my nation,
thwarted my bargains, cooled my friends, heated mine enemies.
And what's his reason ? I am a Jew. Hath not a Jew eyes ?
Hath not a Jew hands, organs, dimensions, senses, affections,
passions, fed with the same food, hurt with the same weapons,
subject to the same diseases, healed by the same means, warmed
and cooled by the same winter and summer, as a Christian is ?
If you prick us, do we not bleed ? If you tickle us, do we not
laugh ? If you poison us, do we not die ? And if you wrong us,
shall we not revenge ? If we are like you in the rest, we will
resemble you in that. If a Jew wrong a Christian, what is his
humility ? Revenge. If a Christian wrong a Jew, what should
his sufferance be by Christian example ? Why, revenge. The
villainy you teach me I will execute ; and it shall go hard but I
will better the instruction.   62

Enter a MAN *from* ANTONIO.

MAN. Gentlemen, my master Antonio is at his house, and desires
to speak with you both.
SALER. We have been up and down to seek him.

Enter TUBAL.

SOLAN. Here comes another of the tribe ; a third cannot be match'd,
unless the devil himself turn Jew.
                                            [*exeunt* SOLANIO, SALERIO, *and* MAN.
SHY. How now, Tubal, what news from Genoa ? Hast thou found
my daughter ?
TUB. I often came where I did hear of her, but cannot find her.   71
SHY. Why there, there, there, there ! A diamond gone, cost me
two thousand ducats in Frankfort ! The curse never fell upon
our nation till now ; I never felt it till now. Two thousand ducats
in that, and other precious, precious jewels. I would my daughter
were dead at my foot, and the jewels in her ear ; would she were
hears'd at my foot, and the ducats in her coffin ! No news of
them ? Why, so—and I know not what's spent in the search.
Why, thou—loss upon loss ! The thief gone with so much, and
so much to find the thief ; and no satisfaction, no revenge ; nor
no ill luck stirring but what lights o' my shoulders ; no sighs but
o' my breathing ; no tears but o' my shedding !   83
TUB. Yes, other men have ill luck too : Antonio, as I heard in Genoa—
SHY. What, what, what ? Ill luck, ill luck ?
TUB. Hath an argosy cast away coming from Tripolis.
SHY. I thank God, I thank God. Is it true, is it true ?
TUB. I spoke with some of the sailors that escaped the wreck.   90
SHY. I thank thee, good Tubal. Good news, good news—ha, ha !—
heard in Genoa.
TUB. Your daughter spent in Genoa, as I heard, one night, fourscore
ducats.
SHY. Thou stick'st a dagger in me—I shall never see my gold again.
Fourscore ducats at a sitting ! Fourscore ducats !   97

59

TUB. There came divers of Antonio's creditors in my company to
Venice that swear he cannot choose but break.
SHY. I am very glad of it; I'll plague him, I'll torture him; I am glad
of it.
TUB. One of them showed me a ring that he had of your daughter for
a monkey.
SHY. Out upon her! Thou torturest me, Tubal. It was my
turquoise; I had it of Leah when I was a bachelor; I would not
have given it for a wilderness of monkeys.
TUB. But Antonio is certainly undone.   107
SHY. Nay, that's true; that's very true. Go, Tubal, fee me an
officer; bespeak him a fortnight before. I will have the heart
of him, if he forfeit; for, were he out of Venice, I can make what
merchandise I will. Go, Tubal, and meet me at our synagogue;
go, good Tubal; at our synagogue, Tubal.   [exeunt.

SCENE II. *Belmont. Portia's house.*

Enter BASSANIO, PORTIA, GRATIANO, NERISSA, *and all their* TRAINS.

SCENE 14
*Exterior. Belmont.
Day.*

POR. I pray you tarry; pause a day or two
Before you hazard; for, in choosing wrong,
I lose your company; therefore forbear a while.
There's something tells me—but it is not love—
I would not lose you; and you know yourself   5
Hate counsels not in such a quality.
But lest you should not understand me well—
And yet a maiden hath no tongue but thought—
I would detain you here some month or two
Before you venture for me. I could teach you   10
How to choose right, but then I am forsworn;
So will I never be; so may you miss me;
But if you do, you'll make me wish a sin,
That I had been forsworn. Beshrew your eyes!
They have o'erlook'd me and divided me;   15
One half of me is yours, the other half yours—
Mine own, I would say; but if mine, then yours,
And so all yours. O! these naughty times
Puts bars between the owners and their rights;
And so, though yours, not yours. Prove it so,   20
Let fortune go to hell for it, not I.
I speak too long, but 'tis to peize the time,
To eke it, and to draw it out in length,
To stay you from election.
BASS.   Let me choose;
For as I am, I live upon the rack.   25
POR. Upon the rack, Bassanio? Then confess
What treason there is mingled with your love.
BASS. None but that ugly treason of mistrust
Which makes me fear th' enjoying of my love;
There may as well be amity and life   30
'Tween snow and fire as treason and my love.
POR. Ay, but I fear you speak upon the rack,
Where men enforced do speak anything.
BASS. Promise me life, and I'll confess the truth.

POR. Well then, confess and live.
BASS.   ' Confess ' and ' love '   35
Had been the very sum of my confession.
O happy torment, when my torturer
Doth teach me answers for deliverance !
But let me to my fortune and the caskets.
POR. Away, then ; I am lock'd in one of them.   40
If you do love me, you will find me out.
Nerissa and the rest, stand all aloof ;
Let music sound while he doth make his choice ;
Then, if he lose, he makes a swan-like end,
Fading in music.   That the comparison   45
May stand more proper, my eye shall be the stream
And wat'ry death-bed for him.   He may win ;
And what is music then ?   Then music is
Even as the flourish when true subjects bow
To a new-crowned monarch ; such it is   50
As are those dulcet sounds in break of day
That creep into the dreaming bridegroom's ear
And summon him to marriage.   Now he goes,
With no less presence, but with much more love,
Than young Alcides when he did redeem   55
The virgin tribute paid by howling Troy
To the sea-monster.   I stand for sacrifice ;
The rest aloof are the Dardanian wives,
With bleared visages come forth to view
The issue of th' exploit.   Go, Hercules !   60
Live thou, I live.   With much much more dismay
I view the fight than thou that mak'st the fray.

A Song, the whilst BASSANIO *comments on the caskets to himself.*

Tell me where is fancy bred,
Or in the heart or in the head,
How begot, how nourished ?   65
Reply, reply.
It is engend'red in the eyes,
With gazing fed ; and fancy dies
In the cradle where it lies.
Let us all ring fancy's knell :   70
I'll begin it—Ding, dong, bell.
ALL.   Ding, dong, bell.
BASS. So may the outward shows be least themselves,
The world is still deceiv'd with ornament.
In law, what plea so tainted and corrupt   75
But, being season'd with a gracious voice,
Obscures the show of evil ?   In religion,
What damned error but some sober brow
Will bless it, and approve it with a text,
Hiding the grossness with fair ornament ?   80
There is no vice so simple but assumes
Some mark of virtue on his outward parts.
How many cowards, whose hearts are all as false
As stairs of sand, wear yet upon their chins
The beards of Hercules and frowning Mars ;   85

Who, inward search'd, have livers white as milk !
And these assume but valour's excrement
To render them redoubted.   Look on beauty
And you shall see 'tis purchas'd by the weight,
Which therein works a miracle in nature,   90
Making them lightest that wear most of it ;
So are those crisped snaky golden locks
Which make such wanton gambols with the wind
Upon supposed fairness often known
To be the dowry of a second head—   95
The skull that bred them in the sepulchre.
Thus ornament is but the guiled shore
To a most dangerous sea ; the beauteous scarf
Veiling an Indian beauty ; in a word
The seeming truth which cunning times put on   100
To entrap the wisest.   Therefore, thou gaudy gold,
Hard food for Midas, I will none of thee ;
Nor none of thee, thou pale and common drudge
'Tween man and man ; but thou, thou meagre lead,
Which rather threaten'st than dost promise aught,   105
Thy plainness moves me more than eloquence,
And here choose I.   Joy be the consequence !
POR. [aside.] How all the other passions fleet to air,
As doubtful thoughts, and rash-embrac'd despair,
And shudd'ring fear, and green-ey'd jealousy !   110
O love, be moderate, allay thy ecstasy,
In measure rain thy joy, scant this excess !
I feel too much thy blessing.   Make it less,
For fear I surfeit.
BASS. [opening the leaden casket.]   What find I here ?
Fair Portia's counterfeit !   What demi-god   115
Hath come so near creation ?   Move these eyes ?
Or whether riding on the balls of mine
Seem they in motion ?   Here are sever'd lips,
Parted with sugar breath ; so sweet a bar
Should sunder such sweet friends.   Here in her hairs   120
The painter plays the spider, and hath woven
A golden mesh t' entrap the hearts of men
Faster than gnats in cobwebs.   But her eyes—
How could he see to do them ?   Having made one,
Methinks it should have power to steal both his,   125
And leave itself unfurnish'd.   Yet look how far
The substance of my praise doth wrong this shadow
In underprizing it, so far this shadow
Doth limp behind the substance.   Here's the scroll,
The continent and summary of my fortune.   130
   ' You that choose not by the view,
   Chance as fair and choose as true !
   Since this fortune falls to you,
   Be content and seek no new.
   If you be well pleas'd with this,   135
   And hold your fortune for your bliss,
   Turn to where your lady is
   And claim her with a loving kiss.'

A gentle scroll.   Fair lady, by your leave ;
I come by note, to give and to receive.   140
Like one of two contending in a prize,
That thinks he hath done well in people's eyes,
Hearing applause and universal shout,
Giddy in spirit, still gazing in a doubt
Whether those peals of praise be his or no ;   145
So, thrice-fair lady, stand I even so,
As doubtful whether what I see be true,
Until confirm'd, sign'd, ratified by you.
POR. You see me, Lord Bassanio, where I stand,
Such as I am.   Though for myself alone   150
I would not be ambitious in my wish
To wish myself much better, yet for you
I would be trebled twenty times myself,
A thousand times more fair, ten thousand times more rich,
That only to stand high in your account
I might in virtues, beauties, livings, friends,
Exceed account.   But the full sum of me
Is sum of something which, to term in gross,
Is an unlesson'd girl, unschool'd, unpractis'd ;   160
Happy in this, she is not yet so old
But she may learn ;   happier than this,
She is not bred so dull but she can learn ;
Happiest of all is that her gentle spirit
Commits itself to yours to be directed,   165
As from her lord, her governor, her king.
Myself and what is mine to you and yours
Is now converted.   But now I was the lord
Of this fair mansion, master of my servants,
Queen o'er myself ;   and even now, but now,   170
This house, these servants, and this same myself,
Are yours—my lord's.   I give them with this ring,
Which when you part from, lose, or give away,
Let it presage the ruin of your love,
And be my vantage to exclaim on you.   175
BASS. Madam, you have bereft me of all words ;
Only my blood speaks to you in my veins ;
And there is such confusion in my powers
As, after some oration fairly spoke
By a beloved prince, there doth appear   180
Among the buzzing pleased multitude,
Where every something, being blent together,
Turns to a wild of nothing, save of joy
Express'd and not express'd.   But when this ring
Parts from this finger, then parts life from hence ;   185
O, then be bold to say Bassanio's dead !
NER. My lord and lady, it is now our time
That have stood by and seen our wishes prosper
To cry ' Good joy '.   Good joy, my lord and lady !
GRA. My Lord Bassanio, and my gentle lady,   190
I wish you all the joy that you can wish,
For I am sure you can wish none from me ;
And, when your honours mean to solemnize

The bargain of your faith, I do beseech you
Even at that time I may be married too.   195
BASS. With all my heart, so thou canst get a wife.
GRA. I thank your lordship you have got me one.
My eyes, my lord, can look as swift as yours:
You saw the mistress, I beheld the maid;
You lov'd, I lov'd; for intermission   200
No more pertains to me, my lord, than you.
Your fortune stood upon the caskets there,
And so did mine too, as the matter falls;
For wooing here until I sweat again,
And swearing till my very roof was dry   205
With oaths of love, at last—if promise last—
I got a promise of this fair one here
To have her love, provided that your fortune
Achiev'd her mistress.
POR.   Is this true, Nerissa?
NER. Madam, it is, so you stand pleas'd withal.   210
BASS. And do you, Gratiano, mean good faith?
GRA. Yes, faith, my lord.
BASS. Our feast shall be much honoured in your marriage.
GRA. We'll play with them: the first boy for a thousand ducats.
NER. What, and stake down?   217
GRA. No; we shall ne'er win at that sport, and stake down—
But who comes here? Lorenzo and his infidel?
What, and my old Venetian friend, Salerio!

Enter LORENZO, JESSICA, *and* SALERIO, *a messenger from Venice.*

BASS. Lorenzo and Salerio, welcome hither,
If that the youth of my new int'rest here
Have power to bid you welcome. By your leave,
I bid my very friends and countrymen,   225
Sweet Portia, welcome.
POR.   So do I, my lord;
They are entirely welcome.
LOR. I thank your honour. For my part, my lord,
My purpose was not to have seen you here;
But meeting with Salerio by the way,   230
He did entreat me, past all saying nay,
To come with him along.
SALER.   I did, my lord,
And I have reason for it. Signior Antonio
Commends him to you.   [*gives* BASSANIO *a letter.*
BASS.   Ere I ope his letter,
I pray you tell me how my good friend doth.   235
SALER. Not sick, my lord, unless it be in mind;
Nor well, unless in mind; his letter there
Will show you his estate.   [BASSANIO *opens the letter.*
GRA. Nerissa, cheer yond stranger; bid her welcome.
Your hand, Salerio. What's the news from Venice?   240
How doth that royal merchant, good Antonio?
I know he will be glad of our success:
We are the Jasons, we have won the fleece.
SALER. I would you had won the fleece that he hath lost

POR. There are some shrewd contents in yond same paper   245
  That steals the colour from Bassanio's cheek :
  Some dear friend dead, else nothing in the world
  Could turn so much the constitution
  Of any constant man. What, worse and worse!
  With leave, Bassanio : I am half yourself,   250
  And I must freely have the half of anything
  That this same paper brings you.
BASS.   O sweet Portia,
  Here are a few of the unpleasant'st words
  That ever blotted paper! Gentle lady,
  When I did first impart my love to you,   255
  I freely told you all the wealth I had
  Ran in my veins—I was a gentleman ;
  And then I told you true. And yet, dear lady,
  Rating myself at nothing, you shall see
  How much I was a braggart. When I told you   260
  My state was nothing, I should then have told you
  That I was worse than nothing ; for indeed
  I have engag'd myself to a dear friend,
  Engag'd my friend to his mere enemy,
  To feed my means. Here is a letter, lady,   265
  The paper as the body of my friend,
  And every word in it a gaping wound
  Issuing life-blood. But is it true, Salerio ?
  Hath all his ventures fail'd ? What, not one hit ?
  From Tripolis, from Mexico, and England,   270
  From Lisbon, Barbary, and India,
  And not one vessel scape the dreadful touch
  Of merchant-marring rocks ?
SALER.   Not one, my lord.
  Besides, it should appear that, if he had
  The present money to discharge the Jew,   275
  He would not take it. Never did I know
  A creature that did bear the shape of man
  So keen and greedy to confound a man.
  He plies the Duke at morning and at night,
  And doth impeach the freedom of the state,   280
  If they deny him justice. Twenty merchants,
  The Duke himself, and the magnificoes
  Of greatest port, have all persuaded with him ;
  But none can drive him from the envious plea
  Of forfeiture, of justice, and his bond.   285
JES. When I was with him, I have heard him swear
  To Tubal and to Chus, his countrymen,
  That he would rather have Antonio's flesh
  Than twenty times the value of the sum
  That he did owe him ; and I know, my lord,   290
  If law, authority, and power, deny not,
  It will go hard with poor Antonio.
POR. Is it your dear friend that is thus in trouble ?
BASS. The dearest friend to me, the kindest man,
  The best condition'd and unwearied spirit   295
  In doing courtesies ; and one in whom

The ancient Roman honour more appears
Than any that draws breath in Italy.
POR. What sum owes he the Jew?
BASS. For me, three thousand ducats.
POR.   What! no more?   300
Pay him six thousand, and deface the bond;
Double six thousand, and then treble that,
Before a friend of this description
Shall lose a hair through Bassanio's fault.
First go with me to church and call me wife,   305
And then away to Venice to your friend;
For never shall you lie by Portia's side
With an unquiet soul.   You shall have gold
To pay the petty debt twenty times over.
When it is paid, bring your true friend along.   310
My maid Nerissa and myself meantime
Will live as maids and widows.   Come, away;
For you shall hence upon your wedding day.
Bid your friends welcome, show a merry cheer;
Since you are dear bought, I will love you dear.   315
But let me hear the letter of your friend.
BASS. [reads.]   ' Sweet Bassanio, my ships have all miscarried, my
creditors grow cruel, my estate is very low, my bond to the Jew is
forfeit ; and since, in paying it, it is impossible I should live, all
debts are clear'd between you and I, if I might but see you at my
death.   Notwithstanding, use your pleasure ; if your love do not
persuade you to come, let not my letter.'   322
POR. O love, dispatch all business and be gone!
BASS. Since I have your good leave to go away,
I will make haste ; but, till I come again,   325
No bed shall e'er be guilty of my stay,
Nor rest be interposer 'twixt us twain.   [exeunt.

SCENE III.   Venice.   A street.   SCENE 15
                                                   Exterior. Venice.
Enter SHYLOCK, SOLANIO, ANTONIO, and GAOLER.   Bridge. Night.

SHY. Gaoler, look to him.   Tell not me of mercy—
This is the fool that lent out money gratis.
Gaoler, look to him.
ANT.   Hear me yet, good Shylock.
SHY. I'll have my bond ; speak not against my bond.
I have sworn an oath that I will have my bond.   5
Thou call'dst me dog before thou hadst a cause,
But, since I am a dog, beware my fangs;
The Duke shall grant me justice.   I do wonder,
Thou naughty gaoler, that thou art so fond
To come abroad with him at his request.   10
ANT. I pray thee hear me speak.
SHY. I'll have my bond.   I will not hear thee speak;
I'll have my bond ; and therefore speak no more.
I'll not be made a soft and dull-ey'd fool,
To shake the head, relent, and sigh, and yield,   15
To Christian intercessors.   Follow not;

I'll have no speaking ; I will have my bond.   [exit.
SOLAN. It is the most impenetrable cur
    That ever kept with men.
ANT.   Let him alone ;
    I'll follow him no more with bootless prayers.   20
    He seeks my life ; his reason well I know :
    I oft deliver'd from his forfeitures
    Many that have at times made moan to me ;
    Therefore he hates me.
SOLAN.   I am sure the Duke
    Will never grant this forfeiture to hold.   25
ANT. The Duke cannot deny the course of law ;
    For the commodity that strangers have
    With us in Venice, if it be denied,
    Will much impeach the justice of the state,
    Since that the trade and profit of the city   30
    Consisteth of all nations.   Therefore, go.
    These griefs and losses have so bated me
    That I shall hardly spare a pound of flesh
    To-morrow to my bloody creditor.
    Well, gaoler, on ; pray God Bassanio come   35
    To see me pay his debt, and then I care not.   [exeunt.

SCENE IV.   Belmont.   Portia's house.

Enter PORTIA, NERISSA, LORENZO, JESSICA, and BALTHASAR.

LOR. Madam, although I speak it in your presence,
    You have a noble and a true conceit
    Of godlike amity, which appears most strongly
    In bearing thus the absence of your lord.
    But if you knew to whom you show this honour,   5
    How true a gentleman you send relief,
    How dear a lover of my lord your husband,
    I know you would be prouder of the work
    Than customary bounty can enforce you.
POR. I never did repent for doing good,   10
    Nor shall not now ; for in companions
    That do converse and waste the time together,
    Whose souls do bear an equal yoke of love,
    There must be needs a like proportion
    Of lineaments, of manners, and of spirit,   15
    Which makes me think that this Antonio,
    Being the bosom lover of my lord,
    Must needs be like my lord.   If it be so,
    How little is the cost I have bestowed
    In purchasing the semblance of my soul   20
    From out the state of hellish cruelty !
    This comes too near the praising of myself ;
    Therefore, no more of it ; hear other things.
    Lorenzo, I commit into your hands
    The husbandry and manage of my house   25
    Until my lord's return ; for mine own part,
    I have toward heaven breath'd a secret vow

SCENE 16
Exterior. Belmont.
Day.

BALTHASAR exits
immediately.

To live in prayer and contemplation,
Only attended by Nerissa here,
Until her husband and my lord's return.   30
There is a monastery two miles off,
And there we will abide. I do desire you
Not to deny this imposition,
The which my love and some necessity
Now lays upon you.
LOR.   Madam, with all my heart   35
I shall obey you in all fair commands.
POR. My people do already know my mind,
And will acknowledge you and Jessica
In place of Lord Bassanio and myself.
So fare you well till we shall meet again.   40
LOR. Fair thoughts and happy hours attend on you !   LORENZO *exits.*
JES. I wish your ladyship all heart's content.
POR. I thank you for your wish, and am well pleas'd
To wish it back on you.   Fare you well, Jessica.
                    [*exeunt* JESSICA *and* LORENZO.   BALTHASAR *re-enters.*
Now, Balthasar,   45
As I have ever found thee honest-true,
So let me find thee still.   Take this same letter,
And use thou all th' endeavour of a man
In speed to Padua ; see thou render this
Into my cousin's hands, Doctor Bellario ;   50
And look what notes and garments he doth give thee,
Bring them, I pray thee, with imagin'd speed
Unto the traject, to the common ferry
Which trades to Venice.   Waste no time in words,
But get thee gone ; I shall be there before thee.   55
BALTH. Madam, I go with all convenient speed.   [*exit.*
POR. Come on, Nerissa, I have work in hand
That you yet know not of ; we'll see our husbands
Before they think of us.
NER.   Shall they see us ?
POR. They shall, Nerissa ; but in such a habit   60
That they shall think we are accomplished
With that we lack.   I'll hold thee any wager,
When we are both accoutred like young men,
I'll prove the prettier fellow of the two,
And wear my dagger with the braver grace,   65
And speak between the change of man and boy
With a reed voice ; and turn two mincing steps
Into a manly stride ; and speak of frays
Like a fine bragging youth ; and tell quaint lies,
How honourable ladies sought my love,   70
Which I denying, they fell sick and died—
I could not do withal.   Then I'll repent,
And wish for all that, that I had not kill'd them.
And twenty of these puny lies I'll tell,
That men shall swear I have discontinued school   75
About a twelvemonth.   I have within my mind
A thousand raw tricks of these bragging Jacks,
Which I will practise.

Gemma Jones as Portia and Susan Jameson as Nerissa

Bassanio (John Nettles), Gratiano (Kenneth Cranham) and Portia (Gemma Jones)

Shylock (Warren Mitchell) and Antonio (John Franklyn-Robbins), with Gratiano (Kenneth Cranham), Solanio (Alan David) and Bassanio (John Nettles) in the background

Susan Jameson as Nerissa   *Leslee Udwin as Jessica*

Enn Reitel as Launcelot Gobbo and Joe Gladwin as Old Gobbo

Gemma Jones as Portia and Warren Mitchell as Shylock

Kenneth Cranham as Gratiano and Warren Mitchell as Shylock

NER.   Why, shall we turn to men ?
POR. Fie, what a question's that,
If thou wert near a lewd interpreter !   80
But come, I'll tell thee all my whole device
When I am in my coach, which stays for us
At the park gate ; and therefore haste away,
For we must measure twenty miles to-day.   [exeunt.

SCENE V. Belmont. The garden.   SCENE 17
                                                   Exterior. Belmont.
Enter LAUNCELOT and JESSICA.   Dusk.

LAUN. Yes, truly ; for, look you, the sins of the father are to be laid
upon the children ; therefore, I promise you, I fear you. I was
always plain with you, and so now I speak my agitation of the
matter ; therefore be o' good cheer, for truly I think you are
damn'd. There is but one hope in it that can do you any good,
and that is but a kind of bastard hope, neither.   7
JES. And what hope is that, I pray thee ?
LAUN. Marry, you may partly hope that your father got you not—
that you are not the Jew's daughter.   10
JES. That were a kind of bastard hope indeed ; so the sins of my
mother should be visited upon me.
LAUN. Truly then I fear you are damn'd both by father and mother ;
thus when I shun Scylla, your father, I fall into Charybdis, your
mother ; well, you are gone both ways.   15
JESS. I shall be sav'd by my husband ; he hath made me a Christian.
LAUN. Truly, the more to blame he ; we were Christians enow before,
e'en as many as could well live one by another. This making of
Christians will raise the price of hogs ; if we grow all to be pork-
eaters, we shall not shortly have a rasher on the coals for money.

Enter LORENZO.

JES. I'll tell my husband, Launcelot, what you say ; here he comes.
LOR. I shall grow jealous of you shortly, Launcelot, if you thus get
my wife into corners.   26
JES. Nay, you need nor fear us, Lorenzo ; Launcelot and I are out ;
he tells me flatly there's no mercy for me in heaven, because I am
a Jew's daughter ; and he says you are no good member of the
commonwealth, for in converting Jews to Christians you raise the
price of pork.
LOR. I shall answer that better to the commonwealth than you can
the getting up of the negro's belly ; the Moor is with child by
you, Launcelot.   34
LAUN. It is much that the Moor should be more than reason ; but if
she be less than an honest woman, she is indeed more than I
took her for.   37
LOR. How every fool can play upon the word ! I think the best
grace of wit will shortly turn into silence, and discourse grow
commendable in none only but parrots. Go in, sirrah ; bid them
prepare for dinner.   41
LAUN. That is done, sir ; they have all stomachs.
LOR. Goodly Lord, what a wit-snapper are you ! Then bid them
prepare dinner.
LAUN. That is done too, sir, only ' cover ' is the word.   45

LOR. Will you cover, then, sir ?
LAUN. Not so, sir, neither ; I know my duty.
LOR. Yet more quarrelling with occasion ! Wilt thou show the
whole wealth of thy wit in an instant ? I pray thee understand a
plain man in his plain meaning : go to thy fellows, bid them
cover the table, serve in the meat, and we will come in to dinner.
LAUN. For the table, sir, it shall be serv'd in ; for the meat, sir, it
shall be cover'd ; for your coming in to dinner, sir, why, let it be
as humours and conceits shall govern. [exit.
LOR. O dear discretion, how his words are suited !   56
The fool hath planted in his memory
An army of good words ; and I do know
A many fools that stand in better place,
Garnish'd like him, that for a tricksy word   60
Defy the matter. How cheer'st thou, Jessica ?
And now, good sweet, say thy opinion,
How dost thou like the Lord Bassanio's wife ?
JES. Past all expressing. It is very meet
The Lord Bassanio live an upright life,   65
For, having such a blessing in his lady,
He finds the joys of heaven here on earth ;
And if on earth he do not merit it,
In reason he should never come to heaven.
Why, if two gods should play some heavenly match,   70
And on the wager lay two earthly women,
And Portia one, there must be something else
Pawn'd with the other ; for the poor rude world
Hath not her fellow.
LOR.   Even such a husband
Hast thou of me as she is for a wife.   75
JES. Nay, but ask my opinion too of that.
LOR. I will anon ; first let us go to dinner.
JES. Nay, let me praise you while I have a stomach.
LOR. No, pray thee, let it serve for table-talk ;
Then howsome'er thou speak'st, 'mong other things   80
I shall digest it.
JES. Well, I'll set you forth.   [exeunt.

ACT FOUR.

SCENE I. *Venice. The court of justice.*

Enter the DUKE, *the* MAGNIFICOES, ANTONIO, BASSANIO, GRATIANO,
SALERIO, *and* OTHERS.

SCENE 18
*Interior. Venice.
A Court. Day.*
The DUKE enters the
assembled court.

DUKE. What, is Antonio here ?
ANT. Ready, so please your Grace.
DUKE. I am sorry for thee ; thou art come to answer
A stony adversary, an inhuman wretch,
Uncapable of pity, void and empty   5
From any dram of mercy.
ANT.   I have heard
Your Grace hath ta'en great pains to qualify
His rigorous course ; but since he stands obdurate,
And that no lawful means can carry me

Out of his envy's reach, I do oppose   10
My patience to his fury, and am arm'd
To suffer with a quietness of spirit
The very tyranny and rage of his.
DUKE. Go one, and call the Jew into the court.
SALER. He is ready at the door ; he comes, my lord.   15

                        Enter SHYLOCK.

DUKE. Make room, and let him stand before our face.
Shylock, the world thinks, and I think so too,
That thou but leadest this fashion of thy malice
To the last hour of act ; and then, 'tis thought,
Thou'lt show thy mercy and remorse, more strange   20
Than is thy strange apparent cruelty ;
And where thou now exacts the penalty,
Which is a pound of this poor merchant's flesh,
Thou wilt not only loose the forfeiture,
But, touch'd with human gentleness and love,   25
Forgive a moiety of the principal,
Glancing an eye of pity on his losses,
That have of late so huddled on his back—
Enow to press a royal merchant down,
And pluck commiseration of his state   30
From brassy bosoms and rough hearts of flint,
From stubborn Turks and Tartars, never train'd
To offices of tender courtesy.
We all expect a gentle answer, Jew.
SHY. I have possess'd your Grace of what I purpose,   35
And by our holy Sabbath have I sworn
To have the due and forfeit of my bond.
If you deny it, let the danger light
Upon your charter and your city's freedom.
You'll ask me why I rather choose to have   40
A weight of carrion flesh than to receive
Three thousand ducats.   I'll not answer that,
But say it is my humour—is it answer'd ?
What if my house be troubled with a rat,
And I be pleas'd to give ten thousand ducats   45
To have it ban'd ?   What, are you answer'd yet ?
Some men there are love not a gaping pig ;
Some that are mad if they behold a cat ;
And others, when the bagpipe sings i' th' nose,
Cannot contain their urine ; for affection,   50
Mistress of passion, sways it to the mood   Line 51: For
Of what it likes or loathes.   Now, for your answer :   'Mistress of passion'
As there is no firm reason to be rend'red   read 'Master of
Why he cannot abide a gaping pig ;   passion'
Why he, a harmless necessary cat ;   55
Why he, a woollen bagpipe, but of force
Must yield to such inevitable shame
As to offend, himself being offended ;
So can I give no reason, nor I will not,
More than a lodg'd hate and a certain loathing   60
I bear Antonio, that I follow thus

A losing suit against him. Are you answered ?
BASS. This is no answer, thou unfeeling man,
  To excuse the current of thy cruelty.
SHY. I am not bound to please thee with my answers.   65
BASS. Do all men kill the things they do not love ?
SHY. Hates any man the thing he would not kill ?
BASS. Every offence is not a hate at first.
SHY. What, wouldst thou have a serpent sting thee twice ?
ANT. I pray you, think you question with the Jew.   70
  You may as well go stand upon the beach
  And bid the main flood bate his usual height ;
  You may as well use question with the wolf,
  Why he hath made the ewe bleat for the lamb;
  You may as well forbid the mountain pines   75
  To wag their high tops and to make no noise
  When they are fretten with the gusts of heaven ;
  You may as well do anything most hard
  As seek to soften that—than which what's harder ?—
  His Jewish heart. Therefore, I do beseech you,   80
  Make no moe offers, use no farther means,
  But with all brief and plain conveniency
  Let me have judgment, and the Jew his will.
BASS. For thy three thousand ducats here is six.
SHY. If every ducat in six thousand ducats   85
  Were in six parts, and every part a ducat,
  I would not draw them ; I would have my bond.
DUKE. How shalt thou hope for mercy, rend'ring none ?
SHY. What judgment shall I dread, doing no wrong ?
  You have among you many a purchas'd slave,   90
  Which, like your asses and your dogs and mules,
  You use in abject and in slavish parts,
  Because you bought them ; shall I say to you
  ' Let them be free, marry them to your heirs—
  Why sweat they under burdens ?—let their beds   95
  Be made as soft as yours, and let their palates
  Be season'd with such viands ' ? You will answer
  ' The slaves are ours '. So do I answer you :
  The pound of flesh which I demand of him
  Is dearly bought, 'tis mine, and I will have it.   100
  If you deny me, fie upon your law !
  There is no force in the decrees of Venice.
  I stand for judgment ; answer ; shall I have it ?
DUKE. Upon my power I may dismiss this court,
  Unless Bellario, a learned doctor,   105
  Whom I have sent for to determine this,
  Come here to-day.
SALER.   My lord, here stays without
  A messenger with letters from the doctor,
  New come from Padua.
DUKE. Bring us the letters ; call the messenger.   110
BASS. Good cheer, Antonio ! What, man, courage yet !
  The Jew shall have my flesh, blood, bones, and all,
  Ere thou shalt lose for me one drop of blood.
ANT. I am a tainted wether of the flock,

Meetest for death ; the weakest kind of fruit   115
Drops earliest to the ground, and so let me.
You cannot better be employ'd, Bassanio,
Than to live still, and write mine epitaph.
  Enter NERISSA, *dressed like a lawyer's clerk.*
DUKE. Came you from Padua, from Bellario ?
NER. From both, my lord. Bellario greets your Grace.   120
                                  [*presents a letter.*
BASS. Why dost thou whet thy knife so earnestly ?
SHY. To cut the forfeiture from that bankrupt there.
GRA. Not on thy sole, but on thy soul, harsh Jew,
  Thou mak'st thy knife keen ; but no metal can,
  No, not the hangman's axe, bear half the keenness   125
  Of thy sharp envy. Can no prayers pierce thee ?
SHY. No, none that thou hast wit enough to make.
GRA. O, be thou damn'd, inexecrable dog !
  And for thy life let justice be accus'd.
  Thou almost mak'st me waver in my faith,   130
  To hold opinion with Pythagoras
  That souls of animals infuse themselves
  Into the trunks of men. Thy currish spirit
  Govern'd a wolf who, hang'd for human slaughter,
  Even from the gallows did his fell soul fleet,   135
  And, whilst thou layest in thy unhallowed dam,
  Infus'd itself in thee ; for they desires
  Are wolfish, bloody, starv'd, and ravenous.
SHY. Till thou canst rail the seal from off my bond,
  Thou but offend'st thy lungs to speak so loud ;   140
  Repair thy wit, good youth, or it will fall
  To cureless ruin. I stand here for law.
DUKE. This letter from Bellario doth commend
  A young and learned doctor to our court.
  Where is he ?
NER.   He attendeth here hard by   145
  To know your answer, whether you'll admit him.
DUKE. With all my heart. Some three or four of you
  Go give him courteous conduct to this place.
  Meantime, the court shall hear Bellario's letter.   149
CLERK. [*reads.*] ' Your Grace shall understand that at the receipt
  of your letter I am very sick ; but in the instant that your
  messenger came, in loving visitation was with me a young doctor
  of Rome—his name is Balthazar. I acquainted him with the cause
  in controversy between the Jew and Antonio the merchant ; we
  turn'd o'er many books together ; he is furnished with my
  opinion which, bettered with his own learning—the greatness
  whereof I cannot enough commend—comes with him at my
  importunity to fill up your Grace's request in my stead. I
  beseech you let his lack of years be no impediment to let him
  lack a reverend estimation, for I never knew so young a body with
  so old a head. I leave him to your gracious acceptance, whose
  trial shall better publish his commendation.'   161

  Enter PORTIA *for* BALTHAZAR, *dressed like a Doctor of Laws.*
DUKE. You hear the learn'd Bellario, what he writes ;

And here, I take it, is the doctor come.
Give me your hand ; come you from old Bellario ?
POR. I did, my lord.
DUKE.   You are welcome ; take your place. 165
Are you acquainted with the difference
That holds this present question in the court ?
POR. I am informed throughly of the cause.
Which is the merchant here, and which the Jew ?
DUKE. Antonio and old Shylock, both stand forth.   170
POR. Is your name Shylock ?
SHY.   Shylock is my name.
POR. Of a strange nature is the suit you follow ;
Yet in such rule that the Venetian law
Cannot impugn you as you do proceed.
You stand within his danger, do you not ?   175
ANT. Ay, so he says.
POR.   Do you confess the bond ?
ANT. I do.
POR.   Then must the Jew be merciful.
SHY. On what compulsion must I ? Tell me that.
POR. The quality of mercy is not strain'd ;
It droppeth as the gentle rain from heaven   180
Upon the place beneath. It is twice blest :
It blesseth him that gives and him that takes.
'Tis mightiest in the mightiest ; it becomes
The throned monarch better than his crown ;
His sceptre shows the force of temporal power,   185
The attribute to awe and majesty,
Wherein doth sit the dread and fear of kings ;
But mercy is above this sceptred sway,
It is enthroned in the hearts of kings,
It is an attribute to God himself ;   190
And earthly power doth then show likest God's
When mercy seasons justice. Therefore, Jew,
Though justice be thy plea, consider this—
That in the course of justice none of us
Should see salvation ; we do pray for mercy,   195
And that same prayer doth teach us all to render
The deeds of mercy. I have spoke thus much
To mitigate the justice of thy plea,
Which if thou follow, this strict court of Venice
Must needs give sentence 'gainst the merchant there.   200
SHY. My deeds upon my head ! I crave the law,
The penalty and forfeit of my bond.
POR. Is he not able to discharge the money ?
BASS. Yes ; here I tender it for him in the court ;
Yea, twice the sum ; if that will not suffice,   205
I will be bound to pay it ten times o'er
On forfeit of my hands, my head, my heart ;
If this will not suffice, it must appear
That malice bears down truth. And, I beseech you,
Wrest once the law to your authority ;   210
To do a great right do a little wrong,
And curb this cruel devil of his will.

POR. It must not be ; there is no power in Venice
Can alter a decree established ;
'Twill be recorded for a precedent,   215
And many an error, by the same example,
Will rush into the state ; it cannot be.
SHY. A Daniel come to judgment ! Yea, a Daniel !
O wise young judge, how I do honour thee !
POR. I pray you, let me look upon the bond.   220
SHY. Here 'tis, most reverend Doctor ; here it is.
POR. Shylock, there's thrice thy money off'red thee.
SHY. An oath, an oath ! I have an oath in heaven.
Shall I lay perjury upon my soul ?
No, not for Venice.
POR.   Why, this bond is forfeit ;   225
And lawfully by this the Jew may claim
A pound of flesh, to be by him cut off
Nearest the merchant's heart. Be merciful.
Take thrice thy money ; bid me tear the bond.
SHY. When it is paid according to the tenour.   230
It doth appear you are a worthy judge ;
You know the law ; your exposition
Hath been most sound ; I charge you by the law,
Whereof you are a well-deserving pillar,
Proceed to judgment. By my soul I swear   235
There is no power in the tongue of man
To alter me. I stay here on my bond.
ANT. Most heartily I do beseech the court
To give the judgment.
POR.   Why then, thus it is :
You must prepare your bosom for his knife.   240
SHY. O noble judge ! O excellent young man !
POR. For the intent and purpose of the law
Hath full relation to the penalty,
Which here appeareth due upon the bond.
SHY. 'Tis very true. O wise and upright judge,   245
How much more elder art thou than thy looks !
POR. Therefore, lay bare your bosom.
SHY.   Ay, his breast—
So says the bond ; doth it not, noble judge ?
' Nearest his heart ', those are the very words.
POR. It is so. Are there balance here to weigh   250
The flesh ?
SHY.   I have them ready.
POR. Have by some surgeon, Shylock, on your charge,
To stop his wounds, lest he do bleed to death.
SHY. Is it so nominated in the bond ?
POR. It is not so express'd, but what of that ?   255
'Twere good you do so much for charity.
SHY. I cannot find it ; 'tis not in the bond.
POR. You, merchant, have you anything to say ?
ANT. But little : I am arm'd and well prepar'd.
Give me your hand Bassanio ; fare you well.   260
Grieve not that I am fall'n to this for you,
For herein Fortune shows herself more kind

Gratiano (Kenneth Cranham), Shylock (Warren Mitchell), Salerio (John Rhys-Davies) and Bassanio (John Nettles)

Than is her custom. It is still her use
To let the wretched man outlive his wealth,
To view with hollow eye and wrinkled brow   265
An age of poverty ; from which ling'ring penance
Of such misery doth she cut me off.
Commend me to your honourable wife ;
Tell her the process of Antonio's end ;
Say how I lov'd you ; speak me fair in death ;   270
And, when the tale is told, bid her be judge
Whether Bassanio had not once a love.
Repent not you that you shall lose your friend,
And he repents not that he pays your debt ;
For if the Jew do cut but deep enough,   275
I'll pay it instantly with all my heart.
BASS. Antonio, I am married to a wife
Which is as dear to me as life itself ;
But life itself, my wife, and all the world,
Are not with me esteem'd above thy life ;   280
I would lose all, ay, sacrifice them all
Here to this devil, to deliver you.
POR. Your wife would give you little thanks for that,
If she were by to hear you make the offer,
GRA. I have a wife who I protest I love ;   285
I would she were in heaven, so she could
Entreat some power to change this currish Jew.
NER. 'Tis well you offer it behind her back ;
The wish would make else an unquiet house.
SHY. [aside.] These be the Christian husbands ! I have a daughter—
Would any of the stock of Barrabas   291
Had been her husband, rather than a Christian !—
We trifle time ; I pray thee pursue sentence.
POR. A pound of that same merchant's flesh is thine.
The court awards it and the law doth give it.   295
SHY. Most rightful judge !
POR. And you must cut this flesh from off his breast.
The law allows it and the court awards it.
SHY. Most learned judge ! A sentence ! Come, prepare.
POR. Tarry a little ; there is something else.   300
This bond doth give thee here no jot of blood :
The words expressly are ' a pound of flesh '.
Take then thy bond, take thou thy pound of flesh ;
But, in the cutting it, if thou dost shed
One drop of Christian blood, thy lands and goods   305
Are, by the laws of Venice, confiscate
Unto the state of Venice.
GRA. O upright judge ! Mark, Jew. O learned judge
SHY. Is that the law ?
POR.   Thyself shalt see the act ;
For, as thou urgest justice, be assur'd   310
Thou shalt have justice, more than thou desir'st.
GRA. O learned judge ! Mark, Jew. A learned judge
SHY. I take this offer then : pay the bond thrice,
And let the Christian go.
BASS.   Here is the money.

POR. Soft!   315
  The Jew shall have all justice. Soft! No haste.
  He shall have nothing but the penalty.
GRA. O Jew! an upright judge, a learned judge!
POR. Therefore, prepare thee to cut off the flesh.
  Shed thou no blood, nor cut thou less nor more   320
  But just a pound of flesh; if thou tak'st more
  Or less than a just pound—be it but so much
  As makes it light or heavy in the substance,
  Or the division of the twentieth part
  Of one poor scruple; nay, if the scale do turn   325
  But in the estimation of a hair—
  Thou diest, and all thy goods are confiscate.
GRA. A second Daniel, a Daniel, Jew!
  Now, infidel, I have you on the hip.
POR. Why doth the Jew pause? Take thy forfeiture.   330
SHY. Give me my principal, and let me go.
BASS. I have it ready for thee; here it is.
POR. He hath refus'd it in the open court;
  He shall have merely justice, and his bond.
GRA. A Daniel still say I, a second Daniel!   335
  I thank thee, Jew, for teaching me that word.
SHY. Shall I not have barely my principal?
POR. Thou shalt have nothing but the forfeiture
  To be so taken at thy peril, Jew.
SHY. Why, then the devil give him good of it!   340
  I'll stay no longer question.
POR.   Tarry, Jew.
  The law hath yet another hold on you.
  It is enacted in the laws of Venice,
  If it be proved against an alien
  That by direct or indirect attempts   345
  He seek the life of any citizen,
  The party 'gainst the which he doth contrive
  Shall seize one half his goods; the other half
  Comes to the privy coffer of the state;
  And the offender's life lies in the mercy   350
  Of the Duke only, 'gainst all other voice.
  In which predicament, I say, thou stand'st;
  For it appears by manifest proceeding
  That indirectly, and directly too,
  Thou hast contrived against the very life   355
  Of the defendant; and thou hast incurr'd
  The danger formerly by me rehears'd.
  Down, therefore, and beg mercy of the Duke.
GRA. Beg that thou mayst have leave to hang thyself;
  And yet, thy wealth being forfeit to the state,   360
  Thou hast not left the value of a cord;
  Therefore thou must be hang'd at the state's charge.
DUKE. That thou shalt see the difference of our spirit,
  I pardon thee thy life before thou ask it.
  For half thy wealth, it is Antonio's;   365
  The other half comes to the general state,
  Which humbleness may drive unto a fine.

POR. Ay, for the state ; not for Antonio.
SHY. Nay, take my life and all, pardon not that.
   You take my house when you do take the prop   370
   That doth sustain my house ; you take my life
   When you do take the means whereby I live.
POR. What mercy can you render him, Antonio ?
GRA. A halter gratis ; nothing else, for God's sake !
ANT. So please my lord the Duke and all the court   375
   To quit the fine for one half of his goods ;
   I am content, so he will let me have
   The other half in use, to render it
   Upon his death unto the gentleman
   That lately stole his daughter—   380
   Two things provided more : that, for this favour,
   He presently become a Christian ;
   The other, that he do record a gift,
   Here in the court, of all he dies possess'd
   Unto his son Lorenzo and his daughter.   385
DUKE. He shall do this, or else I do recant
   The pardon that I late pronounced here.
POR. Art thou contented, Jew ?   What dost thou say ?
SHY. I am content.
POR.   Clerk, draw a deed of gift.
SHY. I pray you, give me leave to go from hence ;   390
   I am not well ; send the deed after me
   And I will sign it.
DUKE.   Get thee gone, but do it.
GRA. In christ'ning shalt thou have two god-fathers ;
   Had I been judge, thou shouldst have had ten more,
   To bring thee to the gallows, not to the font.   [exit SHYLOCK.   The court begins to
DUKE. Sir, I entreat you home with me to dinner.   disperse.
POR. I humbly do desire your Grace of pardon ;
   I must away this night toward Padua,
   And it is meet I presently set forth.
DUKE. I am sorry that your leisure serves you not.   400
   Antonio, gratify this gentleman,
   For in my mind you are much bound to him.
           [exeunt DUKE, MAGNIFICOES, and TRAIN.
BASS. Most worthy gentleman, I and my friend
   Have by your wisdom been this day acquitted
   Of grievous penalties ; in lieu whereof   405
   Three thousand ducats, due unto the Jew,
   We freely cope your courteous pains withal.
ANT. And stand indebted, over and above,
   In love and service to you evermore.
POR. He is well paid that is well satisfied,   410
   And I, delivering you, am satisfied,
   And therein do account myself well paid.
   My mind was never yet more mercenary.
   I pray you, know me when we meet again ;
   I wish you well, and so I take my leave.   415
BASS. Dear sir, of force I must attempt you further ;
   Take some remembrance of us, as a tribute,
   Not as fee.   Grant me two things, I pray you,

Not to deny me, and to pardon me.
POR. You press me far, and therefore I will yield.   420
[*to Antonio.*]   Give me your gloves, I'll wear them for your sake.
[*to Bassanio.*]   And, for your love, I'll take this ring from you.
Do not draw back your hand ; I'll take no more.
And you in love shall not deny me this.
BASS. This ring, good sir—alas, it is a trifle ;   425
I will not shame myself to give you this.
POR. I will have nothing else but only this
And now, methinks, I have a mind to it.
BASS. There's more depends on this than on the value.
The dearest ring in Venice will I give you,   430
And find it out by proclamation ;
Only for this, I pray you, pardon me.
POR. I see, sir, you are liberal in offers ;
You taught me first to beg, and now, methinks,
You teach me how a beggar should be answer'd.   435
BASS. Good sir, this ring was given me by my wife ;
And, when she put it on, she made me vow
That I should neither sell, nor give, nor lose it.
POR. That 'scuse serves many men to save their gifts.
An if your wife be not a mad woman,   440
And know how well I have deserv'd this ring,
She would not hold out enemy for ever
For giving it to me.   Well, peace be with you !
                                   [*exeunt* PORTIA *and* NERISSA.
ANT. My Lord Bassanio, let him have the ring.
Let his deservings, and my love withal,   445
Be valued 'gainst your wife's commandment.
BASS. Go, Gratiano, run and overtake him ;
Give him the ring, and bring him, if thou canst,
Unto Antonio's house.   Away, make haste.   [*exit* GRATIANO.
Come, you and I will thither presently ;   450
And in the morning early will we both
Fly toward Belmont.   Come, Antonio.   [*exeunt.*

SCENE II.   *Venice.   A street.*

Enter PORTIA *and* NERISSA.

POR. Inquire the Jew's house out, give him this deed,
And let him sign it ; we'll away tonight,
And be a day before our husbands home.
This deed will be well welcome to Lorenzo.

Enter GRATIANO.

GRA. Fair sir, you are well o'erta'en.   5
My Lord Bassanio, upon more advice,
Hath sent you here this ring, and doth entreat
Your company at dinner.
POR.   That cannot be.
His ring I do accept most thankfully,
And so, I pray you, tell him.   Furthermore,   10
I pray you show my youth old Shylock's house.

SCENE 19
Exterior. Venice.
Day.

GRA. That will I do.
NER.   Sir, I would speak with you.
    [*aside to Portia.*]   I'll see if I can get my husband's ring,
    Which I did make him swear to keep for ever.
POR. [*to Nerissa.*]   Thou mayst, I warrant.   We shall have old
    swearing
    That they did give the rings away to men ;
    But we'll outface them, and outswear them too.
    [*aloud.*]   Away, make haste, thou know'st where I will tarry.
NER. Come, good sir, will you show me to this house ?   [*exeunt.*

ACT FIVE.

SCENE I. *Belmont. The garden before Portia's house.*

Enter LORENZO *and* JESSICA.

SCENE 20
*Exterior. Belmont.
Night.*

LOR. The moon shines bright.   In such a night as this,
    When the sweet wind did gently kiss the trees,
    And they did make no noise—in such a night,
    Troilus methinks mounted the Troyan walls,
    And sigh'd his soul toward the Grecian tents,   5
    Where Cressid lay that night.
JES.   In such a night
    Did Thisby fearfully o'ertrip the dew,
    And saw the lion's shadow ere himself,
    And ran dismayed away.
LOR.   In such a night
    Stood Dido with a willow in her hand   10
    Upon the wild sea-banks, and waft her love
    To come again to Carthage.
JES.   In such a night
    Medea gathered the enchanted herbs
    That did renew old Æson.
LOR.   In such a night
    Did Jessica steal from the wealthy Jew,   15
    And with an unthrift love did run from Venice
    As far as Belmont.
JES.   In such a night
    Did young Lorenzo swear he lov'd her well,
    Stealing her soul with many vows of faith,
    And ne'er a true one.
LOR.   In such a night   20
    Did pretty Jessica, like a little shrew,
    Slander her love, and he forgave it her.
JES. I would out-night you, did nobody come ;
    But, hark, I hear the footing of a man.

Enter STEPHANO.

LOR. Who comes so fast in silence of the night ?   25
STEPH. A friend.
LOR. A friend !   What friend ?   Your name, I pray you, friend ?
STEPH. Stephano is my name, and I bring word
    My mistress will before the break of day
    Be here at Belmont ; she doth stray about   30

By holy crosses, where she kneels and prays
For happy wedlock hours.
LOR.   Who comes with her?
STEPH. None but a holy hermit and her maid.
I pray you, is my master yet return'd?
LOR. He is not, nor we have not heard from him.   35
But go we in, I pray thee, Jessica.
And ceremoniously let us prepare
Some welcome for the mistress of the house.

Enter LAUNCELOT.

LAUN. Sola, sola! wo ha, ho! sola, sola!
LOR. Who calls?   40
LAUN. Sola! Did you see Master Lorenzo? Master Lorenzo!
Sola, sola!
LOR. Leave holloaing, man. Here!
LAUN. Sola! Where, where?
LOR. Here!   45
LAUN. Tell him there's a post come from my master with his horn
full of good news; my master will be here ere morning.   [*exit.*
LOR. Sweet soul, let's in, and there expect their coming.
And yet no matter—why should we go in?   50
My friend Stephano, signify, I pray you,
Within the house, your mistress is at hand;
And bring your music forth into the air.   [*exit* STEPHANO.
How sweet the moonlight sleeps upon this bank!
Here will we sit and let the sounds of music   55
Creep in our ears; soft stillness and the night
Become the touches of sweet harmony.
Sit, Jessica. Look how the floor of heaven
Is thick inlaid with patines of bright gold;
There's not the smallest orb which thou behold'st   60
But in his motion like an angel sings,
Still quiring to the young-ey'd cherubins;
Such harmony is in immortal souls,
But whilst this muddy vesture of decay
Doth grossly close it in, we cannot hear it.   65

Enter MUSICIANS.

Come, ho, and wake Diana with a hymn;
With sweetest touches pierce your mistress' ear.
And draw her home with music.   [*music.*
JES. I am never merry when I hear sweet music.
LOR. The reason is your spirits are attentive;   70
For do but note a wild and wanton herd,
Or race of youthful and unhandled colts,
Fetching mad bounds, bellowing and neighing loud,
Which is the hot condition of their blood—
If they but hear perchance a trumpet sound,   75
Or any air of music touch their ears,
You shall perceive them make a mutual stand,
Their savage eyes turn'd to a modest gaze
By the sweet power of music. Therefore the poet
Did feign that Orpheus drew trees, stones, and floods;   80

In the television
production the
musicians do not
enter, but music is
heard off.

Since nought so stockish, hard, and full of rage,
But music for the time doth change his nature.
The man that hath no music in himself,
Nor is not mov'd with concord of sweet sounds,
Is fit for treasons, stratagems, and spoils ;   85
The motions of his spirit are dull as night,
And his affections dark as Erebus.
Let no such man be trusted.   Mark the music.

Enter PORTIA *and* NERISSA.

POR. That light we see is burning in my hall.
How far that little candle throws his beams !   90
So shines a good deed in a naughty world.
NER. When the moon shone, we did not see the candle.
POR. So doth the greater glory dim the less :
A substitute shines brightly as a king
Until a king be by, and then his state   95
Empties itself, as doth an inland brook
Into the main of waters.   Music ! hark !
NER. It is your music, madam, of the house.
POR. Nothing is good, I see, without respect ;
Methinks it sounds much sweeter than by day.   100
NER. Silence bestows that virtue on it, madam.
POR. The crow doth sing as sweetly as the lark
When neither is attended ; and I think
The nightingale, if she should sing by day,
When every goose is cackling, would be thought   105
No better a musician than the wren.
How many things by season season'd are
To their right praise and true perfection !
Peace, ho !   The moon sleeps with Endymion,
And would not be awak'd.   [*music ceases.*
LOR.   That is the voice,   110
Or I am much deceiv'd, of Portia.
POR. He knows me as the blind man knows the cuckoo,
By the bad voice.
LOR.   Dear lady, welcome home.
POR. We have been praying for our husbands' welfare,
Which speed, we hope, the better for our words.   115
Are they return'd ?
LOR.   Madam, they are not yet ;
But there is come a messenger before,
To signify their coming.
POR.   Go in, Nerissa ;
Give order to my servants that they take
No note at all of our being absent hence ;   120
Nor you, Lorenzo ; Jessica, nor you.   [*a tucket sounds.*
LOR. Your husband is at hand ; I hear his trumpet.
We are no tell-tales, madam, fear you not.
POR. This night methinks is but the daylight sick ;
It looks a little paler ; 'tis a day   125
Such as the day is when the sun is hid.

Enter BASSANIO, ANTONIO, GRATIANO, *and their* FOLLOWERS.

BASS. We should hold day with the Antipodes,
    If you would walk in absence of the sun.
POR. Let me give light, but let me not be light,
    For a light wife doth make a heavy husband,   130
    And never be Bassanio so for me ;
    But God sort all ! You are welcome home, my lord.
BASS. I thank you, madam ; give welcome to my friend.
    This is the man, this is Antonio,
    To whom I am so infinitely bound.   135
POR. You should in all sense be much bound to him,
    For, as I hear, he was much bound for you.
ANT. No more than I am well acquitted of.
POR. Sir, you are very welcome to our house.
    It must appear in other ways than words,   140
    Therefore I scant this breathing courtesy.
GRA. [to Nerissa.]   By yonder moon I swear you do me wrong ;
    In faith, I gave it to the judge's clerk.
    Would he were gelt that had it, for my part,
    Since you do take it, love, so much at heart.   145
POR. A quarrel, ho, already ! What's the matter ?
GRA. About a hoop of gold, a paltry ring
    That she did give me, whose posy was
    For all the world like cutler's poetry
    Upon a knife, ' Love me, and leave me not '.   150
NER. What talk you of the posy or the value ?
    You swore to me, when I did give it you,
    That you would wear it till your hour of death,
    And that it should lie with you in your grave ;
    Though not for me, yet for your vehement oaths,   155
    You should have been respective and have kept it.
    Gave it a judge's clerk ! No, God's my judge,
    The clerk will ne'er wear hair on's face that had it.
GRA. He will, an if he live to be a man.
NER. Ay, if a woman live to be a man.   160
GRA. Now by this hand I gave it to a youth,
    A kind of boy, a little scrubbed boy
    No higher than thyself, the judge's clerk,
    A prating boy that begg'd it as a fee ;
    I could not for my heart deny it him.   165
POR. You were to blame, I must be plain with you,
    To part so slightly with your wife's first gift,
    A thing stuck on with oaths upon your finger
    And so riveted with faith unto your flesh.
    I gave my love a ring, and made him swear   170
    Never to part with it, and here he stands ;
    I dare be sworn for him he would not leave it
    Nor pluck it from his finger for the wealth
    That the world masters. Now, in faith, Gratiano,
    You give your wife too unkind a cause of grief ;   175
    An 'twere to me, I should be mad at it.
BASS. [aside.]   Why, I were best to cut my left hand off,
    And swear I lost the ring defending it.
GRA. My Lord Bassanio gave his ring away
    Unto the judge that begg'd it, and indeed   180

Deserv'd it too ; and then the boy, his clerk,
That took some pains in writing, he begg'd mine ;
And neither man nor master would take aught
But the two rings.
POR.   What ring gave you, my lord ?
Not that, I hope, which you receiv'd of me.   185
BASS. If I could add a lie unto a fault,
I would deny it ; but you see my finger
Hath not the ring upon it ; it is gone.
POR. Even so void is your false heart of truth.
By heaven, I will ne'er come in your bed   190
Until I see the ring.
NER.   Nor I in yours
Till I again see mine.
BASS.   Sweet Portia,
If you did know to whom I gave the ring,
If you did know for whom I gave the ring,
And would conceive for what I gave the ring,   195
And how unwillingly I left the ring,
When nought would be accepted but the ring,
You would abate the strength of your displeasure.
POR. If you had known the virtue of the ring,
Or half her worthiness that gave the ring,   200
Or your own honour to contain the ring,
You would not then have parted with the ring.
What man is there so much unreasonable,
It you had pleas'd to have defended it
With any terms of zeal, wanted the modesty   205
To urge the thing held as a ceremony ?
Nerissa teaches me what to believe :
I'll die for't but some woman had the ring.
BASS. No, by my honour, madam, by my soul,
No woman had it, but a civil doctor,   210
Which did refuse three thousand ducats of me,
And begg'd the ring ; the which I did deny him,
And suffer'd him to go displeas'd away—
Even he that had held up the very life
Of my dear friend.   What should I say, sweet lady ? 215
I was enforc'd to send it after him ;
I was beset with shame and courtesy ;
My honour would not let ingratitude
.So much besmear it.   Pardon me, good lady ;
For by these blessed candles of the night,   220
Had you been there, I think you would have begg'd
The ring of me to give the worthy doctor.
POR. Let not that doctor e'er come near my house ;
Since he hath got the jewel that I loved,
And that which you did swear to keep for me,   225
I will become as liberal as you ;
I'll not deny him anything I have,
No, not my body, nor my husband's bed.
Know him I shall, I am well sure of it.
Lie not a night from home ; watch me like Argus ;   230
If you do not, if I be left alone,

Now, by mine honour which is yet mine own,
I'll have that doctor for mine bedfellow.
NER. And I his clerk ; therefore be well advis'd
How you do leave me to mine own protection.   235
GRA. Well, do you so, let not me take him then ;
For, if I do, I'll mar the young clerk's pen.
ANT. I am th' unhappy subject of these quarrels.
POR. Sir, grieve not you ; you are welcome notwithstanding.
BASS. Portia, forgive me this enforced wrong ;   240
And in the hearing of these many friends
I swear to thee, even by thine own fair eyes,
Wherein I see myself——
POR.   Mark you but that !
In both my eyes he doubly sees himself,
In each eye one ; swear by your double self,   245
And there's an oath of credit.
BASS.   Nay, but hear me.
Pardon this fault, and by my soul I swear
I never more will break an oath with thee.
ANT. I once did lend my body for his wealth,
Which, but for him that had your husband's ring,   250
Had quite miscarried ; I dare be bound again,
My soul upon the forfeit, that your lord
Will never more break faith advisedly.
POR. Then you shall be his surety.   Give him this,
And bid him keep it better than the other.   255
ANT. Here, Lord Bassanio, swear to keep this ring.
BASS. By heaven, it is the same I gave the doctor !
POR. I had it of him.   Pardon me, Bassanio,
For, by this ring, the doctor lay with me.
NER. And pardon me, my gentle Gratiano,   260
For that same scrubbed boy, the doctor's clerk,
In lieu of this, last night did lie with me.
GRA. Why, this is like the mending of highways
In summer, where the ways are fair enough.
What, are we cuckolds ere we have deserv'd it ?   265
POR. Speak not so grossly.   You are all amaz'd.
Here is a letter ; read it at your leisure ;
It comes from Padua, from Bellario ;
There you shall find that Portia was the doctor,
Nerissa there her clerk.   Lorenzo here   270
Shall witness I set forth as soon as you,
And even but now return'd ; I have not yet
Enter'd my house.   Antonio, you are welcome ;
And I have better news in store for you
Than you expect.   Unseal this letter soon ;   275
There you shall find three of your argosies
Are richly come to harbour suddenly,
You shall not know by what strange accident
I chanced on this letter.
ANT.   I am dumb.
BASS. Were you the doctor, and I knew you not ?   280
GRA. Were you the clerk that is to make me cuckold ?

NER. Ay, but the clerk that never means to do it,
    Unless he live until he be a man.
BASS. Sweet doctor, you shall be my bedfellow ;
    When I am absent, then lie with my wife.   285
ANT. Sweet lady, you have given me life and living;
    For here I read for certain that my ships
    Are safely come to road.
POR.   How now, Lorenzo !
    My clerk hath some good comforts too for you.
NER. Ay, and I'll give them him without a fee.   290
    There do I give to you and Jessica,
    From the rich Jew, a special deed of gift,
    After his death, of all he dies possess'd of.
LOR. Fair ladies, you drop manna in the way
    Of starved people.
POR.   It is almost morning,   295
    And yet I am sure you are not satisfied
    Of these events at full.   Let us go in,
    And charge us there upon inter'gatories,
    And we will answer all things faithfully.
GRA. Let it be so.   The first inter'gatory   300
    That my Nerissa shall be sworn on is,
    Whether till the next night she had rather stay,
    Or go to bed now, being two hours to day.
    But were the day come, I should wish it dark,
    Till I were couching with the doctor's clerk.
    Well, while I live, I'll fear no other thing
    So sore as keeping safe Nerissa's ring.   [*exeunt.*   **All leave except**
                                                     ANTONIO.

GLOSSARY

Graham May

Difficult phrases are listed under the most important or most difficult word in them. If no such word stands out, they are listed under the first word.

Words appear in the form they take in the text. If they occur in several forms, they are listed under the root form (singular for nouns, infinitive for verbs).

Line references are given only when the same word is used with different meanings, and when there are puns.

Line numbers of prose passages are counted from the last numbered line before the line referred to (since the numbers given do not always correspond to those in this edition).

'A, he, II i 30, II ii 46
ABODE, delay
ABOUT, 'is come about', has changed direction
ABOVE, (i.e. on some form of upper stage, e.g. at a balcony, window, etc.), II vi 25 SD
ABRAM, Abraham; (see THIRD POSSESSOR), I iii 67
ABRIDG'D, 'to be abridg'd', about being reduced
ABROAD, i.e. outside the gaol, III iii 10
A-CAP'RING, a-dancing
ACCOMPLISHED, equipped
ACCORDINGLY, in accord, i.e. dark-skinned and dressed in white like Morocco
ACCOUNT, estimation, III ii 155; calculation, III ii 157
ACCUS'D, see FOR
ACT, performance, IV i 19; legal statute, IV i 309
ADDRESS'D ME, prepared myself
ADO, trouble, difficulty
ADVANTAGE, 'upon advantage', expecting to receive or pay interest
ADVANTAGES, increase, interest
ADVENTURING, hazarding
ADVICE, 'more advice', further consideration
ADVIS'D, cautious, V i 234; 'be advis'd', take careful thought
ADVISED, careful, deliberate
ADVISEDLY, deliberately
AESON, in Greek mythology, the father of Jason (see MEDEA)

AFEARD, AFEAR'D, afraid
AFFECTION, desires related to the will
AFFECTIONS, thoughts and feelings, I i 16; wishes, desires (which prompt passions), III i 50; passions, emotions, V i 87
AGAIN, back again, V i 12; 'sweat again', sweated repeatedly
AGITATION, (probably a blunder for 'cogitation', understanding)
AGUE, acute fever
AIR, i.e. tune, V i 76
ALABASTER, (allusion to the effigies which were common on tombs in churches)
ALACK, Alas; 'Alack the day', Alas
ALBEIT, although
ALCIDES, Hercules; (allusion to the classical myth that Hercules rescued the Trojan princess Hesione from a sea-monster to which she was to be sacrificed. He did this, however, not because he loved her but because he wished to possess the horses which Laomedon, her father and the king of Troy, had promised him as a reward for the rescue; hence Bassanio has 'much more love' than had Hercules), III ii 55
A'LEVEN, eleven
ALL, just, III ii 83; only, nothing but, IV i 316; 'all as', equally (see DULL), II vii 8
ALLAY, temper, qualify, II ii 171; throw away, subdue (with, perhaps, overtones of the meaning 'mix one metal with a baser metal'), III ii 111

ALOOF, at a distance; (standing) at a distance, III ii 58

AM, 'am to learn', see LEARN

A MANY, many

AMAZ'D, bewildered

AMITY, friendship, platonic love

AMOROUS, loving

AN, if; 'an if', if; 'An 'twere to me', If it had been done to me

ANDREW, ('St Andrew' was the name of one of the two very large Spanish galleons whose capture by the English off Cadiz in 1596 caused great excitement)

ANGEL, (allusion to the 'angel', an English gold coin which bore the figure of the archangel Michael treading on the dragon), II vii 56; (i) heavenly angel, (ii) gold 'angel' coin (see above; pun), II vii 58

ANON, immediately, soon

ANSWER (v.), answer for (Lorenzo jests on one's duty to beget children for the good of the commonwealth), III v 32; satisfy, IV i 3

AN'T, if it

ANTIPODES, 'We should hold . . . Antipodes . . . sun', i.e. If you always walked at night it would then be day for us, as it now is on the other side of the world

ANYTHING, see IS, I ii 113; see RACK, III ii 33

APPARENT, clear, manifest (or 'seeming')

APPROPRIATION, addition

APPROVE, prove, confirm

ARGOSIES, see ARGOSY

ARGOSY, merchant vessel of the largest size and burden (especially used to denote those of Ragusa and Venice; perhaps an allusion to the Argo, the boat which the Argonauts rowed on their quest for the Golden Fleece; see GOLDEN FLEECE)

ARGUS, (in classical mythology, a monster with a hundred eyes, only one pair of which slept at any one time, so that he was ever watchful)

ARM'D, i.e. prepared, IV i 259

AS, see WHO, I i 93, I ii 41; Such as, III ii 109; see PAPER, III ii 266

ASPECT, visage

ASSUME, invest myself with, claim, II ix 51

ASSUR'D, sure, satisfied, I iii 25 (see ASSURED)

ASSURED, guaranteed by adequate security (legal term; pun on 'assur'd'), I iii 26

ATTEMPT, urge, IV i 416

ATTEND, see LEISURES, I i 68

ATTENDED, 'When neither is attended', i.e. when each sings on its own, V i 103

ATTRIBUTE TO, visible symbol of, IV i 186; quality or characteristic of, IV i 190

AUGHT, anything

BACKWARD, see GROWS

BADGE, distinctive mark

BAG-PIPER, (bag-pipe music was regarded as being melancholy)

BAIT (n.), 'melancholy bait', bait of melancholy; (v.), act as a bait for, III i 45

BALANCE, scales (regarded as plural)

BALTHAZAR, (in some editions of the Bible, 'Balthazar' appears for 'Belshazzar', the Babylonian name given to Daniel; see Daniel, v 1, and DANIEL)

BAN'D, poisoned

BARBARY, the Saracen countries along the north coast of Africa

BARK (n.), small sailing vessel

BARRABAS, i.e. (i) Barabbas, the criminal whom the Jews asked Pontius Pilate to release instead of Jesus (see Mark xv 6–15), (ii) (perhaps) Barrabas, the villain-hero of Marlowe's Jew of Malta

BASE, (pun: lead is a 'base' metal), II vii 50

BATE, diminish

BATED, (i) dejected, (ii) reduced in weight, III iii 32

BE, are, I ii 19; By, II ii 38; 'be least themselves', see LEAST

BEARD, (Old Gobbo probably mistakes Launcelot's long hair on the back of his head for a beard), II ii 84

BEARS DOWN TRUTH, overthrows righteousness

BECHANC'D, were it to happen

BECOME, (often =) suit, befit

BECOMES, befits

BEEFS, beef-cattle

BEFORE, i.e. early, III i 109

BEHOLDING, beholden, indebted

BEING, 'Being ten . . . gold', see UNDERVALUED

BESHREW, (a mild curse), i.e. 'May evil befall'

BESPEAK, engage beforehand

BEST, i.e. at his best (pun on 'beast', I ii 79), I ii 77; see WERE, II viii 33

BESTOWED, i.e. stowed on board the ship bound for Belmont, II ii 155

BETHINK ME, take careful thought; 'bethink me straight', be put in mind immediately

BETIMES, early, in good time
BETTER, do better than, go beyond, II i 61
BETWEEN, 'between the change . . . boy', i.e. as if I were a boy whose voice was just breaking
BIDDING, i.e. your having first to ask me
BIG, pregnant, full
BLACK MONDAY, Easter Monday (called 'Black' because on that day in 1360 the weather had been so cold that it caused many deaths; dreams occurring on great Church feast days were considered to be especially portentous; see FALLING)
BLAME, 'to blame he', to be blamed is he; 'to blame', too blameworthy, V i 166
BLEARED, tear-blotched
BLENT, blended, confused
BLEST, most blessed, II i 46; 'is twice blest', i.e. bestows a double blessing
BLOOD, 'for the blood', to control the passions (the blood was supposed to be the seat of emotion and passion)
BLOW, 'blow me to an ague', stir up an 'ague' (= acute fever) within me
BLUNT, (i) blunt of edge, (ii) plain-spoken, (iii) base (pun; see DULL)
BODY, see PAPER, III ii 266
BOLD, 'be bold to say', say with confidence
BOND, see SINGLE BOND, I iii 140; 'take his bond', accept his legal pledge
BONDMAN's, see KEY
BONNET, soft cap-like hat
BOOTLESS, unavailing
BOSOM (adj.), intimate, confidential, III iv 17
BOTTOM, ship's hold, ship (probable allusion to the proverb 'Venture not all in one bottom')
BOUGHT, see DEAR, III ii 315
BOUND, i.e. bound by a legal agreement (to be responsible for the repayment of the debt), I ii 4f.; obliged, IV i 65, IV i 402; indebted, V i 135f.; constrained by a legal bond (pun on V i 135), V i 137
BOUNTY, benevolence
BRASS, i.e. as hard, unpitying, as brass
BREAK, fail to fulfil the agreed terms of the loan-contract, I iii 131; see CHOOSE BUT BREAK, III i 99; 'break his day', fail to pay on the due date; 'break up', open (the seal of), II iv 11
BREATH, speech, II ix 90
BREATH'D, uttered
BREATHING COURTESY, utterance of welcome

BRED, see NEAR, II i 3
BREED (n.), offspring, increase, i.e. interest (see I iii 91), I iii 129
BRIEF, 'In very brief', i.e. To be as brief as one can be
BROTHERS, see WOULD
BRUTUS' PORTIA, see PORTIA
BUILDS, see MARTLET, WEATHER
BURGHERS, citizens
BUSHELS (a 'bushel' is a measure of capacity equal to eight gallons)
BUT, (often =) only, merely; see HOLD, I i 77; i.e. with respect to whom (I do not), I ii 98; except, III i 81; see DULL, III ii 163; i.e. that does not, V i 61; were it not for, V i 250; 'But I should', Without my being forced to, I i 26; 'touching but', if they merely touched; 'but even now worth this', i.e. just a moment ago worth all this concern (or 'of so great value'); 'spend but', only waste; 'but assumes', that it does not take on itself; 'even now, but now', i.e. at this very moment; 'so old But she may', i.e. too old to be able to; 'But now', Just now, III ii 168; 'but some woman had', if some woman was not given
BY, concerning, I ii 49; For, to imply, II ix 26; see LIVE, III v 18

CANDLE, see HOLD, LIGHT (adj.), II vi 41
CANDLES, i.e. stars
CARRION, (i) worthless beast (term of abuse), (ii) reference to Shylock's fleshly nature (see FLESH AND BLOOD), III i 31; 'carrion Death', a loathsome figure of Death made like a corrupting body, i.e. 'Death's Head' ('carrion = (i) pertaining to corrupting flesh, (ii) loathsome; see DEATH'S HEAD)
CAST AWAY, i.e. destroyed, lost
CASUALTY, mischance
CATER-COUSINS, good friends (perhaps from 'cater' = supply food, i.e. 'cater-cousins' = fellow bread-eaters; no blood-relationship is implied)
CATO'S DAUGHTER, see PORTIA
CAUSE, legal case, IV i 168
CERECLOTH, waxed cloth used for embalming, shroud
CEREMONY, see URGE
CERTAIN, determined, fixed, IV i 60
CERTIFIED, informed, assured, guaranteed
CHANCE AS FAIR, Hazard as fortunately
CHANGE, see BETWEEN, III iv 66
CHARGE (n.), see ON, IV i 252; (v.) command, IV i 233; 'charge us . . . inter'gator-

90

ies', question us upon oath (witnesses at court were called on oath ('charged') to answer a series of questions ('interrogatories'))

CHARTER, i.e. a legal document granting the freedom and guaranteeing the constitution of the state of Venice

CHARYBDIS, see SCYLLA

CHEER (n.), countenance, III ii 314

CHEER'ST, 'How cheer'st thou', How are you, what cheer

CHILD, 'child that shall be', (probably an allusion to second childhood, or to Launcelot's intention of being a good son henceforth)

CHILDHOOD, see PROOF

CHOOSE, i.e. do what you please, I ii 42; 'choose but break', avoid going bankrupt

CHUS, (a name probably derived from *Genesis* x 6)

CIRCUMSTANCE, elaborate reasoning, circumlocution

CIVIL DOCTOR, doctor of civil law (perhaps a pun on 'civil' = polite)

CIVILITY, see OBSERVANCE OF CIVILITY

CLEAR, pure, unsullied, II ix 42

CLOSE, (adj.), secret, II vi 47; (v.), see MUDDY, V i 65

COIN, see ANGEL

COLCHOS', Colchis's (see GOLDEN FLEECE)

COLD, 'your suit is cold', your request is refused, your wooing unsuccessful (common idiom: 'cold' = (i) without power to move or influence, (ii) (perhaps) 'dead' (pun)), II vii 73

COLT, i.e. young and foolish person (pun: in Shakespeare's day the Neapolitans were renowned for their horsemanship)

COME, 'come into the court and swear', i.e. bear me witness on oath; 'is come about', has changed direction; 'come near', see CREATION

COMES, 'comes sooner by', sooner gets

COMING-IN, 'simple coming-in', modest income (with bawdy innuendo)

COMMANDED, 'be commanded that command', i.e. be servants who are now masters

COMMEND, 'commend me', send my greetings

COMMENDS (n.), commendations, II ix 90; (v.), 'Commends him', Sends his greetings, III ii 234

COMMODITY, merchandise, I i 178; commercial privileges, benefits, III iii 27

COMMON, public, III iv 53

COMPETENCY, moderate means

COMPLEXION, (allusion to the fact that Devils were often represented as black in Shakespeare's day), I ii 116; (i) temperament, (ii) appearance, II vii 79; nature, disposition, III i 26

COMPROMIS'D, agreed

CONCEIT, understanding, thought, I i 92; conception, III iv 2

CONCEITS, see HUMOURS

CONCEIVE, understand

CONDITION, character, disposition, I ii 116

CONDITION'D, natured

CONDUCT, escort

CONFESS, see RACK, III ii 26; acknowledge, IV i 176; 'confess and live', (a reversal of the proverbial 'Confess and be hanged' alluding to the practice of allowing confession and absolution before execution)

CONFISCATE, confiscated

CONFOUND, destroy

CONFUSIONS, see TRY

CONJURED, conveyed (as a magician would summon up or control spirits)

CONSCIENCE, see FIEND, II ii 5

CONSTANT, steadfast, with a settled and well-ordered constitution, III ii 249

CONSTITUTION, state of mind

CONTAIN, retain, V i 201

CONTINENT, container, summary

CONTINUANCE, 'grant continuance', allow me to persevere in

CONTRARY, wrong, I ii 85

CONTRIVE, plot

CONTRIVED, plotted

CONVENIENCY, convenience, fitness

CONVENIENT, due, appropriate

CONVENIENTLY, properly

CONVERTED, (legal word used of property changed from separate to joint ownership)

COPE, 'cope . . . withal', give as an equivalent for the trouble you have been to so courteously and charitably

COSTLY, lavish, rich

COUNSEL, 'good counsel the cripple', wisdom, which is an old man incapable of action

COUNTERFEIT, portrait

COUNTY, Count

COURT, see COME, I ii 63

COURTESIES, acts of Christian kindness

COURTESY, act of Christian kindness, IV i 33; see BREATHING COURTESY, V i 141; 'for a Christian courtesy', as an act of Christian benevolence

91

COUSIN'S, kinsman's

COVER, i.e. lay the table-cloth (Launcelot puns on 'cover' = cover the head with a hat, and the fact that he should remove his hat out of respect for Lorenzo), III v 45f., III v 51; 'should cover . . . bare', should wear their hats who now bare their heads (in deference to social superiors), i.e. should be masters who now are servants

COVER'D, i.e. served in covered dishes

COZEN, deceive

CRADLE, (i) i.e. eyes (where it was born), (ii) (its) infancy

CREAM, 'cream and mantle', cover with a pale and sour froth (i.e. acquire a set, grave, expression); see SORT

CREATION, 'Hath come so near creation', Has painted a portrait that is (i) so nearly indistinguishable from the person herself, (ii) so lifelike that it is almost equivalent to the creation of a real human being

CREDIT, 'of credit', to be believed

CRESSID, Cressida (see TROILUS)

CRIPPLE, see COUNSEL

CRISPED, curled

CROSS (v.), i.e. (i) make the sign of the cross (at the end of a prayer), (ii) thwart, hinder, III i 18

CROSSES, wayside crosses (common both in England and in Italy)

CROSSING, 'crossing . . . highway of talk', i.e. departing from plain speech

CROST, crossed, i.e. thwarted, unfortunate

CUPID, classical blind boy-god of love

CUR, dog

CURELESS, incurable

CURRENT, i.e. tenor, drift

CURRISH, doglike; (see WOLF), IV i 133

CURTSY, (i) do obeisance, (ii) i.e. bob up and down on the waves

CUT, see ALABASTER, I i 84

CUTLER'S POETRY . . . KNIFE, i.e. the sort of poetry a maker of cutlery would inscribe on a knife (doggerel verses were frequently inscribed on cutlery)

DAM, mother, III i 26; mother (a contemptuous term usually used for quadrupeds), IV i 136

DAMN, see WOULD, I i 98

DANGER (n.), 'within his danger', in his power (or 'in his debt'); (v.), harm, damage, IV i 38

DANIEL, (allusion to the story of Susannah and the Elders told in the Apocrypha (Susanna, v 45ff.): when the Elders accused Susannah, the youthful Daniel acted as judge and prevented a miscarriage of justice by revealing that the witness and accusers were corrupt; Gratiano realises (III iv 328) that Daniel succeeded in turning the tables on the accusers just as Portia does; see BALTHAZAR)

DARDANIAN, Trojan

DEAL, (large) amount

DEAR, see WORTH, I i 62; searly (pun), III ii 315; 'dear bought', obtained at a high price

DEATH, see CARRION

DEATH'S HEAD, i.e. a *memento mori* (a picture or carving of a skull, perhaps with cross-bones, used to remind the living of the inevitability of death, and often carved on contemporary tombstones)

DEBATING OF, considering within myself the size of

DEED, i.e. deed of gift (there is a pun on this at IV ii 4), IV ii 1

DEEDS, see UPON, IV i 201

DEFACE, destroy

DEFECT, (blunder for 'effect' = import)

DEFY, disdain, set at nought

DEGREES, social ranks

DELIBERATE, calculating

DEMI-GOD, i.e. god-like painter (see CREATION)

DENY, refuse to accept, hinder, III iii 26; 'deny this imposition', refuse this charge, command

DEPENDING, see IMPOSITION

DEPENDS, 'There's more depends . . . value', i.e. More than the cost of the ring is at stake

DERIV'D, inherited, gained

DESERV'D, see WHY, V i 265

DESTINIES, see FATES

DIANA, Roman goddess of the moon, of chastity, and of hunting

DIDO, Queen of Carthage. (The Latin poet Virgil, in his *Aeneid*, tells how, after the fall of Troy at the hands of the Greeks, Aeneas and the escaping Trojans were shipwrecked on Dido's shores. Through the plotting of Venus (the goddess of love), Dido fell in love with Aeneas, and tried to persuade him to live with her in Carthage. But Aeneas was ordered by the gods to abandon her and leave to found his own nation in Italy. After his departure, Dido killed herself, and was cremated on a giant funeral pyre)

DIFFERENCE, dispute, IV i 166
DIMENSIONS, bodily frame
DIRECTION, guidance, instruction, II i 14; 'direction for', i.e. instructions on how to draw up
DISABLING, disparagement, undervaluing
DISCHARGE, settle his obligation to, III ii 275
DISCONTINUED, 'discontinued . . . twelve-month', been out of school at least a year (ironic)
DISCOVER, reveal
DISCOVERY, see OFFICE
DISCRETION, 'dear discretion', precious discrimination (ironic)
DISPATCH, swiftly conclude
DIVERS, several
DIVINE, clergyman
DIVISION, see SUBSTANCE
DO, see WITHAL, III iv 72; 'do them reverence', make obeisance to them
DOCTOR, see CIVIL DOCTOR, V i 210
DOG, (it was proverbial that dogs barked at a person in disgrace or at a disadvantage) I i 94
DOIT, trifling sum (originally a small Dutch coin)
DOUBLE, see DOUBLY, V i 245; 'double ducats', see DUCATS
DOUBLET, coat, upper garment
DOUBLY, i.e. (i) in a double reflection, (ii) deceitful (pun)
DOUBT, see OUT, I i 21, I i 155
DOUBTFUL, fearful, III ii 109
DOWRY, 'the dowry . . . head', the possession, endowment, of another's head (i.e. a wig)
DRAM, i.e. smallest amount
DRAW, take, receive, IV i 87; draw up, IV i 389
DREAD AND FEAR, power to inspire dread and fear
DREAM, 'dream of money-bags', (it was considered to be unlucky to dream of money, although dreams were also considered to be notoriously ambiguous)
DREW, i.e. enchanted with his music
DRIVE, reduce, IV i 367
DRONES, non-working male honey-bees (hence 'sluggards')
DROSS, see SHOWS
DRUDGE, see PALE
DUCAT, a Venetian gold coin worth somewhere between a quarter and a half of a contemporary English pound sterling
DUCATS, see DUCAT (3000 ducats would

have approximately equalled 700 to 1500 contemporary English pounds sterling, i.e. at least £20,000 in modern money; a substantial sum); 'double ducats', coins of twice the value of ordinary ducats
DUKE, (often =) Duke (or 'Doge') of Venice
DULL, (i) gloomy, obscure, (ii) blunt of edge (pun on 'blunt'; see BLUNT), II vii 8; inert, drowsy, V i 86; 'so dull but she can', i.e. so stupid that she cannot
DULL-EY'D, i.e. easily deceived
DUMB-SHOW, theatrical entertainment in which no words were spoken
DUTY, see COVER
DWELL, remain, I iii 150

EANING, lambing
EANLINGS, new-born lambs
EAT, 'eat . . . drink . . . pray with you', (i.e. Shylock regards these three activities as sacramental acts)
EDGE, 'edge of a feather bed', i.e. some sexual escapade (or perhaps 'getting married')
EKE, augment, increase
ELECTION, choice, II ix 3; making the choice, III ii 24
ELSE NOTHING, nothing else
EMBRACE, 'embrace th' occasion', take advantage of the opportunity ('occasion')
ENDYMION, (in Greek mythology, a shepherd loved by the moon-goddess Diana who caused him to be cast into a perpetual sleep in a cave in Mount Latmos; Portia probably draws attention to Jessica lying with Lorenzo on the moonlit bank)
ENFORCE, urge upon
ENGEND'RED, (the eyes were believed to be the initial entry-way through which love first entered the soul)
ENOW, enough
ENTER, see MIND, II viii 42
ENTERTAIN, maintain, keep up
ENTIRELY, sincerely, heartily
ENVIOUS, malicious
ENVY'S, malice's
EQUAL, exact, I iii 144; matched, equivalent, III iv 13
ERE, before; 'ere himself', i.e. before she saw the lion itself
EREBUS, the gloomy cavern underground through which the dead had to walk on their way to Hades (the Underworld of classical mythology)
ERGO, therefore (a pedantic latinism)

93

ERROR, injustice, miscarriage of justice

ESTATE, wealth (see UPON), I i 43; wealth, I i 123; condition, situation, III ii 238

ESTATES, social ranks, (or) property, possessions

ESTIMATION, valuation, II vii 26; 'But in the estimation . . . hair', Only by a hair's breadth on the scale, or a hair's weight

EVEN, see BUT, I i 35; impartial, II vii 25; 'even now, but now', i.e. at this very moment

EVER, always, constantly, I ii 24; always, II v 4, II ix 71

EVERMORE, continually

EVERY, 'every man . . . man', see MAN

EXCEEDING, exceedingly

EXCESS, interest, I iii 57; (i) violence of passion, (ii) interest, usury (pun), III ii 112

EXCHANGE, i.e. change into boy's clothes

EXCLAIM ON, accuse, reproach

EXCREMENT, outgrowth (often used of hairs), i.e. (mere) external attributes

EXHIBIT MY TONGUE, (probably blunder for 'inhibit my speech'; it could, however, mean, 'demonstrate what my tongue would say')

EXHORTATION, sermon (perhaps an allusion to the practice of Puritan preachers who often gave sermons of great length)

EXPECT, await, V i 48

EXTREMEST MEANS, uttermost financial resources

EYE, sight, view, i.e. presence, I i 137; sight, II v 41; i.e. tears, III ii 46

FAIR, see STOOD, II i 20

FAIRLY, properly, fitly, honourably (perhaps 'completely')

FAITHLESS, unbelieving

FALL, befall, I ii 79; i.e. be considered as, I iii 75; give birth to, I iii 83

FALLING, 'falling out that year . . . afternoon', (hopelessly jumbled details given in parody of the customary style of prognostications)

FALLS, turns out, III ii 203

FALSE, i.e. treacherous, III ii 83

FANCY, love, fond affection, III ii 63

FASHION, see REASONING, I ii 18; pretence, IV i 18

FAST, secure; 'Fast bind . . . find', (proverbial)

FASTER, more firmly, III ii 123

FATES, (in Greek mythology, the 'Fates' were three goddesses who controlled the destinies of men by spinning the thread of life; they were Clotho, who spun the thread, Lachesis, who measured it out, and Atropos, who cut it)

FATHER, (a common form of address by a younger person to an old man: it would not necessarily reveal Launcelot's identity to Old Gobbo), II ii 55ff.; (future) father-in-law, II vi 25

FAWNING PUBLICAN, servilely ingratiating, flattering, publican (scornful allusion (i) to 'Publicani', the Roman taxgatherers (Antonio therefore being likened by Shylock to an oppressive taxgatherer stealing Shylock's rightful profits), (ii) to the 'Publican' in the parable of the Publican and the Sinner (see Luke xviii 10–14) who fawned on God when praying for mercy (i.e., Shylock implies, just as Antonio is ingratiating himself with Shylock in asking him for a loan)

FEAR, doubt, be apprehensive about, III ii 29; fear for, III v 2; be concerned about, V i 306

FEAR'D, terrified, II i 9

FEARFUL, timid (or 'untrustworthy, and therefore arousing anxiety in me')

FEE, 'fee me an officer', hire a Sheriff's officer (or 'catchpole', whose duty it was to make arrests)

FEIGN, artistically portray

FELL, (adj.), cruel, IV i 135; (v.), befell, I ii 79

FELLOW, see FLIGHT, I i 141; equal, III v 74

FETCHING MAD BOUNDS, gambolling, bounding madly

FIE, (for) shame (exclamation of disgust or contempt)

FIELDS, battle-fields, battles

FIEND, (Launcelot Gobbo visualises himself as the central character in a morality-play in which the devil ('the fiend') and 'conscience' strive for the mastery over Launcelot's soul), II ii 2ff.)

FILL-HORSE, draught horse which draws in 'fills' (= shafts)

FLAT, shallows

FLATS, shoals (stretches of sand covered by a thin film of water)

FLEECE, see GOLDEN FLEECE, III ii 243; (pun on 'fleets'), III ii 244

FLEET, fade, vanish

FLESH AND BLOOD, (i) kindred, child, III i 30; (ii) sensual appetites and passions (Solanio quibbles on (i)), III i 31

FLIDGE, fledged, ready and able to fly

FLIGHT, 'his fellow . . . flight', an arrow

identical ('fellow') to the first, of the same size and weight, equally feathered, and of the same power of flight

FLOOD, sea; 'main flood', high tide

FLOOR, 'floor of heaven', (possible allusion to the fact that the underside of the canopy over the stage may have been painted with stars and other heavenly bodies)

FLOURISH, a fanfare; sound a fanfare, II i o Stage Direction

FOLLOW, pursue, IV i 172; persevere in, IV i 199

FOLLOWING, see SO

FOLLOWS, 'follows . . . instructions', practises what he preaches

FOND, foolish

FOOL, foolish, II ix 26; 'Still more fool . . . here', i.e. The longer I stay here, the bigger fool I shall appear to be

FOOT (n.), i.e. path, II iv 35; (v.), kick, I iii 113

FOOTING, footsteps

FOPP'RY, foolishness

FOR, because, I iii 37; see LOVE, I iii 165; as for, II viii 41, III v 52f., IV i 365; see COURTESY, III i 41; i.e. as if she were, IV i 161 Stage Direction; 'for that', because, I iii 38; 'For the heavens', In heaven's name; 'for all this', i.e. despite all that Shylock has said, II v 39; 'for him', on his account, II viii 50; 'for money', at any price; 'for thy life . . . accus'd', let justice be called into question because you are still allowed to live; 'for the state . . . Antonio', that is with respect to the state's portion, but not that of Antonio; 'for him', on his behalf, V i 172; 'For giving', Because you gave

FORCE, power, II ix 30; 'of force', through necessity, IV i 56; of necessity, IV i 416

FORE-SPURRER, one who gallops ahead

FORFEIT (n.), penalty (for failure to comply with the terms of the contract), I iii 143; (v.) i.e. fail to fulfil his part of the bargain and hence be liable to pay the penalty

FORFEITURE, penalty, forfeit, I iii 159; legal process to exact a penalty when a bond for debt becomes forfeit, i.e. 'forfeiture to hold' = penalty to be considered legally valid and to be exacted, III iii 25

FORFEITURES, penalties exacted when bonds became forfeit

FORM, image, likeness

FORSWORN, 'am forsworn', would have broken my promise

FORTH, i.e. taking place, in hand, I i 15; out, I i 143

FORTUNE, often personified as a woman blindfolded so that she would be impartial; 'in fortune of my choice', in my luck when I choose; 'Fortune to', May good luck attend

FRAM'D, created

FRANKFORT, (an international fair was held at Frankfort twice a year)

FRAUGHT, laden (with goods)

FREEDOM, see IMPEACH, III ii 280

FRETTEN, fretted, chafed, vexed

FROM, by, III ii 166; away from, V i 230

FRUTIFY, (blunder for 'certify' or 'notify')

FULL STOP, i.e. the 'stop' or halt in the manage of a trained horse (Solanio's tongue is bolting)

FULSOME, rank (i.e. in heat)

FURNISH, supply, I iii 53; 'furnish thee', equip, finance you (so that you may go)

GABERDINE, loose upper garment of coarse material

GAG'D, pledg'd, bound

'GAINST, see VOICE, IV i 351

GAPING PIG, roasted pig with its mouth open

GARNISH, decoration, dress

GARNISH'D, i.e. furnished (with words; or 'clothed'; see GUARDED)

GAUGE, judge, measure

GEAR, business, purpose, II ii 151; 'for this gear', as a consequence of all this chatter ('gear' = business) of yours

GELT, gelded

GENTLE, noble, tender, II i 12; (pun on 'Gentile', in contrast to the 'faithless Jew' her father), II iv 34; tender, noble person (with pun on 'Gentile'), II vi 50; (pun on 'Gentile'), IV i 34

GETTING UP, i.e. making pregant

GIVE, 'to give . . . receive', i.e. to exchange (kisses and vows of love)

GLEANED, separated (to 'glean' = to gather ears of corn left by the reapers; see SEED)

GLISTERS, glitters ('All that . . . gold' is proverbial)

GLOVES, (gloves were often exchanged as tokens of affection)

GO, 'it shall go hard but', i.e. I shall do my utmost to

GOBBO, (in Italian 'gobbo' = hump-backed)

GOD-FATHERS, (i) god-parents, (ii) (slang) jurors (Gratiano puns on this meaning, IV i 393)

95

GOLDEN FLEECE, (allusion to the Greek myth of Jason, who gathered together the Argonauts to sail the ship *Argo* in quest of the Golden Fleece. He found it in Colchis (a country at the eastern end of the Black Sea), and won it with the help of Medea, the enchantress-daughter of the King of Colchis (who, like Portia's father, confronted the Argonauts with a threefold test of their wisdom)

GONE, lost, damned, III v 15

GOOD, i.e. commercially sound, I iii 13; *see* MAKE, I iii 89

GOODWINS, Goodwin Sands, off the mouth of the Thames

GOSSIP, 'my gossip Report', i.e. Dame Rumour ('gossip' = (originally) godmother, (then) female confidante, (then) tale-teller)

GOT, begot, III v 9

GRACE, 'best grace', highest excellence

GRAMERCY, many thanks (originally 'May God reward you greatly', from the Old French 'grant merci')

GRANDAM, grandmother

GRATIANO, ('Graziano' was the traditional name for the comic doctor in the Italian *Commedia dell'Arte*; *see* PLAY)

GRATIFY, reward

GRATIS, free of charge; i.e. without charging interest, III iii 2

GRAV'D, engraved, inscribed

GRAVEL-BLIND, i.e. totally blind (pun on 'sand-blind'; *see* SAND-BLIND)

GRECIAN TENTS, (i.e. the camp of the Greek army pitched outside the walls of Troy during the Trojan War)

'GREE, agree

GROSS, full amount, I iii 50; *see* TERM, III ii 158

GROW, 'grow to', (used of milk when burnt to the bottom of a saucepan and hence imbued with an unpleasant taste; i.e. 'incline towards lechery'; *see* SMACK), II ii 14

GROWS, 'grows backward', (i) gets shorter instead of longer, (ii) grows at the wrong end (*see* BEARD)

GUARDED, ornamented (e.g. with braid; perhaps an allusion to the 'motley' coat traditionally worn by the fool)

GUDGEON, a small fish easily caught (i.e. 'credulous fool')

GUILED, treacherous

HABIT, (i) behaviour, demeanour, (ii) garb

(pun: 'suit', II ii 186, puns on 'habit'), II ii 175; dress, apparel, III iv 60

HABITATION, dwelling (*see* NAZARITE)

HAD, would have, I ii 12; would, I ii 44

HAGAR'S OFFSPRING, (Hagar was a Gentile and bondwoman to Sarah, Abraham's wife; her son Ishmael was an outcast and a 'wild' man; *see Genesis* xvi 12)

HALTER, hangman's noose

HAND, handwriting, II iv 12; 'of no hand', (probably) neither directly to the right or left

HANG'D, i.e. when he was hanged (*see* WOLF)

HANGING, 'hanging about . . . heart', (i.e. like a timid wife or mistress); 'Hanging and wiving . . . destiny', i.e. Being hanged and choosing a wife are governed purely by destiny (not by personal choice; proverbial)

HANGMAN'S, i.e. executioner's

HAPPIER, more fortunate

HAPPY, Fortunate, III ii 161

HARD, close, IV i 145; hard-hearted, V i 81

HARDLY, with great difficulty

HARE, (allusion to the apparent 'madness' of hares when they gambol about in courtship)

HARMONY, 'Such harmony . . . souls', i.e. This celestial harmony can only be heard by immortal souls

HAT, (hats were worn during dinner)

HAZARD, that which is risked (*see* LATTER HAZARD), I i 151

HE, i.e. Shylock, III ii 279; 'he . . . he . . . he . . .', i.e. one man . . . another man . . . yet another man . . .

HEAD, 'I will ever . . . head', i.e. You will always be a fool

HEARS'D, coffined, buried

HEAVY, i.e. sorrowful (pun), V i 130

HEDG'D, i.e. confined

HEELS, 'with thy heels', (i) indignantly (Elizabethan idiom), (ii) (running away) with my feet (pun)

HENCE, go hence, III ii 313

HELD, *see* URGE, V i 206

HERCULES, a mythical Greek hero of fabulous strength; *see* LICHAS, III i 32; *see* ALCIDES, III ii 60

HIE THEE, hasten

HIGH-DAY, befitting a festival, i.e. high-flown

HIGH TOP, topmast

HIGHWAY, *see* CROSSING

HIP, *see* UPON, I iii 41; 'on the hip', i.e. 'upon the hip' (*see* UPON)

HIRE, wages

HIS, its, I i 141; (i.e. the Christian's), III i 57; (i.e. the Jew's), III i 59; (probably) its, III ii 82; for him, III iii 45; its, IV i 72

HIT, i.e. accurately find, II ii 38; hit the mark, i.e. been successful, III ii 269

HOLD, take this, II iv 19; i.e. offer, III iv 62; 'hold the world . . . world', i.e. (i) consider the world to be no more than what it is (i.e. transitory and of limited value), (or) (ii) take no more interest in the affairs of the world than does the rest of the world; 'hold a candle', i.e. stand by and openly witness (possibly with a bawdy innuendo); 'hold . . . for your bliss', consider . . . to be the source of your happiness; 'hold opinion with', share the opinion of; 'hold day with', see ANTIPODES; 'hold out', i.e. persist

HOLDS, 'That ever holds', That is always the case; 'holds . . . question', is the cause of this present dispute

HONEST, chaste, III v 36

HOOD (n.), 'by my hood', by my masque-hood, (or, ironically) by my monk's hood (using an oath dating from the Middle Ages); (v.), see HAT, II ii 178

HOPE, think, II ii 121

HORN, (i) musical horn (see POST, SOLA), (ii) cornucopia, horn of plenty

HOT TEMPER, impetuous temperament (allusion to the belief that the disposition of a human being depended upon the balance or imbalance within him of four elements or 'humours': blood (hot and wet), phlegm (cold and moist), choler (hot and dry) and melancholy or (black) bile (cold and dry); 'hot temper' would imply an excess of choler or blood)

HOVEL-POST, post supporting a shed

HOW, 'How now', Hello, how are you; 'Yet look how far . . . so far . . .', Yet see how far . . . just so far . . .

HOWLING, wailing, lamenting

HOWSOME'ER, howsoever

HUDDLED, crowded

HUMBLENESS, i.e. humility on your part, IV i 367

HUMILITY, patient endurance

HUMOUR, whim, caprice

HUMOURS AND CONCEITS, inclinations of character and personal opinions

HUSBANDRY, 'husbandry and manage', ordering and management

HYRCANIAN DESERTS, deserts in a desolate area south of the Caspian Sea, famed for its wildness

I'FAITH, in faith, indeed

IMAGIN'D, all imaginable

IMMUR'D, entombed

IMPEACH, 'doth impeach . . . state', i.e. accuses the state of failing to uphold the liberties of its citizens; 'Will much impeach . . . state', Will do much to cause the processes of justice of the state to be called into question

IMPERTINENT, (mistake for 'pertinent')

IMPOSITION, see DENY, III iv 33; 'father's imposition . . . caskets', i.e. the conditions commanded by your father whereby success or failure in wooing you depends entirely upon the (suitor's) choice of caskets (see II i 38–42)

IN, on, I iii 68; by, II ii 22; during, II iv 1; 'in choosing', if you choose

INCARNATION, (blunder for 'incarnate')

INDIAN, i.e. dark-complexioned (the general Elizabethan ideal of feminine beauty seems to have been fairness of complexion)

INEXECRABLE, which cannot sufficiently be execrated

INFECTION, (malapropism for 'affection' = inclination)

INNOCENCE, (i) foolishness, (ii) freedom from moral fault or cunning, i.e. sincerity, (iii) childlike friendship and affection

INSCROLL'D, set down in this scroll (i.e. you would have made a different choice and received a different answer, in the form of a portrait rather than a scroll)

INSCULP'D UPON, (merely) engraved on the surface

INSERTED, (either) (i) introduced into the Bible, (or) (ii) introduced into the conversation by you

INTEREST, i.e. usury, I iii 46

INTER'GATORY, see CHARGE

INTERMISSION, 'intermission . . . than you', I can as little have delay or respite than can you, my lord

INT'REST, (commercial term), see YOUTH, III ii 222

IS, are, I ii 90; 'Is that anything now', i.e. Does what Gratiano has just said actually mean anything

IT, i.e. your 'plots and purposes', I i 136; 'it is a wise father . . . child', (reversal of the proverb 'It is a wise child that knows his own father')

IWIS, certainly

JACKS, fellows (contemptuous)

97

JACOB, 'When Jacob graz'd . . . sheep', *see Genesis* xxx 31–43, I iii 66ff.; *see* THIRD POSSESSOR, I iii 67–9

JACOB'S STAFF, (*see Genesis* xxxii 10, where Jacob contrasts his former poverty (when he first crossed the Jordan he possessed merely a staff) with his present power: 'With my staff came I over this Jordan, and now have I gotten two companies'; see also *Hebrews* xi 21)

JANUS, (the Roman god of exits and entrances often represented as possessing two faces which looked in opposite directions, one to see the future, and one to see the past)

JASONS, *see* GOLDEN FLEECE, I i 172; 'We are the Jasons . . . fleece', *see* I i 169–172

JAUNDICE, yellowness of skin (thought to be caused by an excess of the bodily 'humours', 'choler' or 'yellow bile' (*see* HOT TEMPER)

JESSICA, (a name perhaps derived from 'Iscah' of *Genesis* xi 29; in Hebrew 'Jessica' = spy or looker-out)

JEW, (a type of heartlessness), II ii 103

JOT, small particle

JUMP, agree

JUST, exact, IV i 322

KEEN, savage, cruel, III ii 278

KEEP, if you keep, I i 108; 'keep his day', i.e. repays the loan by the date agreed

KEPT, dwelt, III iii 19

KEY, 'a bondman's key', the tone of voice of a suppliant slave

KIND (adj.) (often =) (i) generous, kindly, (ii) natural; (n.), nature, I iii 80

KINDNESS, *see* WERE, I iii 138

KISS (v.), embrace, pursue, II ix 66; 'kiss her burial', do homage to her place of burial

KNAPP'D GINGER, chewed ginger (perhaps 'nibbled ginger-snaps')

KNAVE, (i) scoundrel, (ii) servant, I iii 171

KNOW, (i) recognise, (ii) i.e. sleep with (pun), V i 229; 'know myself', i.e. have a proper sense of my own identity and worth, command over myself (allusion to the proverbial injunction that one should 'know thyself', and thus ground wisdom in true self-knowledge); 'know me', (i) recognise me, (ii) consider this as an introduction (quibble), IV i 414

LABAN'S, *see* JACOB

LADING, cargo

LATE, recently, IV i 387

LATTER HAZARD, second risk

LAUGH, i.e. next have a merry time together, I i 66

LAUGHABLE, i.e. truly amusing

LAUNCELOT, 'Your worship's . . . Launcelot', i.e. Old Gobbo disclaims the title of 'Master' for his son (*see* MASTER)

LEADEST, carriest, maintainest

LEARN, 'I am to learn', I have yet to find out (i.e. 'I don't know')

LEAST, 'be least themselves', i.e. falsify inner reality

LEAVE, part with, V i 150, V i 172

LEFT, i.e. endowed with wealth (by inheritance), I i 161; parted with, V i 196

LEISURE, 'your leisure . . . not', i.e. that you do not have the leisure to be able to stay

LEISURES, 'We'll make our leisures . . . yours', i.e. We will put ourselves entirely at your disposal ('attend on' your leisure) and consider our doing so to be as pleasurable as if it were done for our own pleasure

LET, 'let him lack', which will deprive him of

LETTERS, i.e. a letter

LEVEL, guess (as one would 'level' (= aim) a gun at its target)

LIBERAL, unrestrained, licentious, II ii 170; (i) generous, (ii) sexually licentious, V i 226

LICHAS, a friend of and attendant upon Hercules (Hercules's wife Deianira instructed Lichas to take the poisoned shirt of Nessus to her husband. Hercules put it on, was fatally poisoned, and, in his violent rage and pain, hurled Lichas far out to sea)

LIEU, return, IV i 405; 'In lieu of this', In return for this

LIFE, *see* FOR, IV i 129

LIGHT (adj.), (i) clear, (ii) wanton, II vi 42; i.e. wanton (pun), V i 129; light in weight (pun), V i 130; (v.), fall, IV i 38

LIGHTEST, (i) most wanton, (ii) lightest in weight (pun)

LIGHTS, falls

LIKE, *see* WILFUL, I i 146; likely, I iii 125; likely, probable, II vii 49

LIKELY, fit, promising

LINE OF LIFE, (in palmistry) the circular line at the base of the thumb

LINEAMENTS, bodily or facial features (or, more probably, 'characteristics', 'temperamental qualities')

LION'S, *see* THISBY

LIVE, 'Live thou', If you live, III ii 61; 'live one by another', (i) dwell side by side with

98

each other, (ii) make a living off one another
LIVER, (regarded as the seat of the emotions)
LIVERIES, livery (see LIVERY)
LIVERS WHITE AS MILK, (the liver and the blood were supposed to be the seats of passion; hence 'white-livered' = cowardly)
LIVERY, distinctive uniform worn by the servants of a particular master; see SHADOW'D, II i 2
LIVING, possessions, V i 286
LIVINGS, possessions
LODG'D, deep-seated
LOOK, 'Look to', Look after, II v 16; attend to, take care of, III i 39; keep careful watch over, III iii 1f.; 'look what', whatever
LOOSE, release, i.e. waive (or 'lose' = forget), IV i 24
LORD, (quibble on 'lady' = wife, 'lord' = husband), II ix 85; 'Lord Love', (i.e. addressed to Cupid; see CUPID)
LOSE, 'They lose it . . . care', (Compare *Matthew* xvi 25: 'For whosoever will save his life shall lose it: and whosoever will lose his life for my sake shall find it')
LOSING, unprofitable
LOTT'RY OF MY DESTINY, game of chance on which my fate depends
LOVE, friend, IV i 272; 'for my love', for my love's sake
LOVER, friend
LOW SIMPLICITY, (either) (i) humble, honest plainness, (or) (ii) base folly

MAGNIFICOES, ('magnifico' was the title bestowed upon the nobles who rule the Venetian state beneath the Doge)
MAID, (probably 'waiting-gentlewoman', i.e. not a common servant)
MAIN FLOOD, high tide; 'main of waters', ocean
MAKE, see MERCHANDISE, III i 111; 'make shift', contrive; 'make interest good', justify the taking of interest; 'make stand', wait
MAN, 'he is everyman . . . man', i.e. although he has all the attributes of other men yet in himself he is nothing
MANAGE, see HUSBANDRY
MANNA, spiritual nourishment ('Manna' was the food miraculously supplied to the Israelites during their progress through the wilderness; see *Exodus* xvi)
MANNERS, character, behaviour, II iii 18
MANTLE, see CREAM
MARK (n.), 'God bless the mark', (probably a

formula to avert an evil omen, hence used by way of apology for mentioning anything horrible, disgusting, or profane); (v.) take careful note (of)
MARRY, indeed (originally an oath: 'By (the Blessed Virgin) Mary')
MARS, Roman god of fertility and war
MART, market-place (i.e. the Rialto)
MARTLET, swift (which builds precarious nests in insecure places)
MASKERS, masquers, actors in the masque (see MASQUE)
MASQUE, amateur dramatic entertainment of the Early Tudor Period, in which masquers wearing masks or other disguises made a formal entry to a dinner accompanied by torchbearers, and, after giving their dramatic entertainment, joined the other guests in a dance)
MASTER, (term of some dignity, usually applied to the employer of a servant, rather than the servant himself; see LAUNCELOT)
MASTERS, possesses
MATCH, bargain, III i 37
MATCH'D, found to match them
MATTER, substance, meaning, III v 61
MEAN, 'seated in the mean', positioned between the extremes of too little and too much
MEANING, 'chooses his meaning', i.e. guesses your father's intention directly
MEANS, see EXTREMEST MEANS, I i 138; financial wealth, resources, I iii 14, III ii 265
MEASURE (n.), 'In measure . . . joy', Pour out your joy moderately (or, if 'rain' = 'rein', 'Control and moderate your joy'); (v.), i.e. travel, III iv 84
MEASURES, paces (allusion to the practice of carefully training horses to perform a formal 'manage')
MEAT, food, III v 51
MEDEA, (in Greek mythology, the sorceress and priestess of Hecate who helped Jason win the Golden Fleece. She helped Jason murder her half-brother Apsyrtus to delay their pursuers, and contrived the death of Jason's enemy Pelias. She restored the youth of Jason's father Aeson by her magic arts. She eventually married Jason, but later he repudiated her in order to marry Glauce; Medea murdered her two children by Jason in revenge and escaped to Athens. See GOLDEN FLEECE)
MEET, fitting, III v 64, IV i 399
MEETEST, most fitting

MENDING, see WHY

MERCHANDISE, trading, I i 40, I i 45; 'make . . . merchandise', drive whatever bargain

MERCHANT-MARRING, destructive to merchant-ships (and merchants)

MERE, utter, absolute, III ii 264

MESHES, nets, snares

METHOUGHTS, It seemed to me

MIDAS, (a legendary King of Phrygia, who requested of the gods that everything he touched might be turned into gold. The wish was granted, but as his food became gold as soon as he touched it, he prayed the gods to take the favour back; he was then ordered to bathe in the Pactolus, and the river ever afterwards rolled over golden sands)

MILLION, i.e. (perhaps) million times

MINCING, see TURN

MIND, see PRESAGES, I i 175; opinion, IV i 402; 'have no mind of', have no desire; 'enter in your mind of love', i.e. Intrude into your thoughts of love; 'have a mind to', i.e. am resolved upon having

MISCARRIED, was destroyed, lost, II viii 29

MISCONST'RED, misconstrued

MISLIKE, Dislike

MISTRUST, doubt, uncertainty

MITIGATE, i.e. temper it with mercy

MOAN, 'make moan', complain (see ABRIDG'D)

MODESTY, sobriety, decorum, II ii 171; see WANTED, V i 205

MOE, more

MOIETY, portion

MONEY, see FOR, III v 20

MONTFERRAT, (the Monferrato family had been powerful and influential in Italy from the end of the tenth to the middle of the sixteenth centuries)

MOON, (Gratiano may or may not be aware that the moon was a symbol of inconstancy), V i 142

MORE, again, II ii 182; 'more than reason', larger than is reasonable (there are several puns here and in following lines on 'Moor' and 'more')

MORROW, morning

MORTAL-BREATHING, mortal and living

MORTIFYING, killing (sighs and groans were thought to draw blood away from the heart and weaken it)

MOTHER, 'his wise mother', i.e. Rebeccah, mother of Jacob (see THIRD POSSESSOR)

MOTIONS, impulses

MOUTHS, 'in our mouths', to be mentioned in our conversation

MUDDY, 'muddy vesture of decay . . . hear it', i.e. mortal flesh does emprison man's immortal soul, we cannot hear the music of the spheres

MURDER, 'murder . . . long', (proverbial)

MUSIC, (i.e. a small orchestra), V i 53, V i 98

MUTTONS, sheep

MUTUAL, common

NARROW SEAS, i.e. the English Channel

NAUGHTY, wicked, good-for-nothing (stronger than the modern sense)

NAZARITE, Nazarene. i.e. Jesus (allusion to the miracle of the Gadarene Swine, when Jesus cast devils from possessed men into a herd of swine (see, e.g., Mark v 1–13)

NEAR, accurate, I iii 49; 'near bred', closely related

NEAT'S, ox's ('neat's tongue' contains a bawdy innuendo = penis)

NECESSARY, i.e. domestically necessary (to keep down mice; 'harmless' and 'necessary' are perhaps to differentiate this cat from a cat which is a witch's familiar), IV i 55

NECESSITY, state of need

NEEDS, of necessity

NEITHER, 'that is but . . . neither', i.e. and that is merely a kind of bastard hope ('neither' emphasise the negative implication of the asseveration)

NERISSA, (a name probably meaning 'dark-haired', being derived from the Italian 'nero' = black)

NESTOR, (the oldest and wisest of the Greek heroes at the siege of Troy)

NEW, newly, again, II ix 49

NICE, (over-) fastidious

NO, not, II ii 41, III ii 145

NOMINATED FOR, i.e. named as

NONE, see WISH, III ii 192; 'will none of', will have nothing to do with

NOR, i.e. And, V i 84; 'Nor will not', i.e. 'speak to lady afterward . . .'; 'nor . . . nor . . .', neither . . . nor . . .

NOSE FELL A-BLEEDING, (supposed to be a sign of bad luck)

NOT, 'not I', i.e. for being forsworn; III ii 21

NOTARY, person publicly authorised to draw up or attest contracts

NOTE, 'by note', (commercial term) by a bill of dues, i.e. by authorisation in writing (the scroll)

NOTHING, 'nothing undervalu'd', in no way inferior
NOUGHT, nothing is, V i 81

O ME, Alas
OBLIGED, pledged (see VENUS' PIGEONS)
OBSCUR'D, hidden, darkened (Lorenzo puns on 'obscur'd' = disguised)
OBSERVANCE OF CIVILITY, respect due to good manners
OCCASION, see EMBRACE, I i 64; see QUARRELLING, III v 48
OCCASIONS, needs, requirements
O'ERLOOK'D, bewitched, looked on with the 'evil eye'
O'ERSTARE, outstare
O'ERTRIP, run swiftly over
OF, (often =) from; see QUESTION, I i 185; between, II v 2; In, II viii 38; 'of force', through necessity
OFFEND, see OFFICES, II ix 61
OFFEND'ST, injurest
OFFER, 'which doth offer', which (i.e. the 'table' or the 'man') does put itself (or 'himself') forward
OFFICE, ''tis an office of discovery', i.e. the whole function of torch-bearing is to bring things into clear view
OFFICES, official functions, positions of authority, II ix 41; acts, duties, IV i 33; 'To offend and judge . . . natures', i.e. An offender cannot judge his own case
OFT, often
OLD, 'With mirth . . . old wrinkles come', i.e. Let mirth and laughter pucker the face into the wrinkles characteristic of old age; 'old swearing', plenty of oaths (colloquial)
ON, 'on your charge', at your expense
ONCE, on this one occasion, IV i 210
ONE NIGHT, in a single night
ON'T, of it
OPE, open; see DOG, I i 94
OPINION, reputation, I i 102; 'opinion of', reputation for
OR . . . OR . . . , either . . . or . . . ; 'Or whether', Or
ORB, planet, heavenly body (allusion to the 'Music of the Spheres'. According to ancient astronomers, the heavenly bodies were fixed on a series of hollow concentric crystalline spheres which rotated around the earth; it was believed that as they turned they made a divinely harmonious music which was inaudible to the ears of ordinary mortals)

ORPHEUS, see POET
OSTENT, appearance, show
OSTENTS, expressions, shows
OTHER, others, I i 54
OUR, my (the Duke uses the 'Royal Plural'), IV i 16, IV i 363
OUT, quarrelling, III v 27; 'out of doubt', undoubtedly, I i 21; (i) doubtless, (ii) because of (needless) doubt (as to my love for you), I i 155; 'Out upon', Shame upon, III i 31, III i 104; 'From out', Out from
OUT-DWELLS HIS HOUR, i.e. is late
OUTFACE THEM, i.e. stubbornly and impudently maintain our story
OUT-NIGHT, i.e. continue, and win, our rivalry in words
OUTSIDE, i.e. surface glitter, (or) the beautiful face that once surrounded the skull
OVER-NAME, i.e. recount their names from one end of the list to the other
OVERPEER, tower over, look down upon
OVER-WEATHER'D, worn or damaged by exposure to the weather (or, perhaps, 'with timbers springing apart'; see SCARFED)

PACK, i.e. be gone
PADUA, (a famous centre for the study of civil law)
PAGE, attendant (i.e. Lichas)
PAGE'S, young male attendant's
PAGEANTS, high mobile stages (something like modern floats) often shaped like castles, ships, etc, mounted on wagons, and used for miracle plays and other entertainments
PAIN, pains, trouble
PALE, 'pale and common drudge', pallid public slave (i.e. silver, when made into coins)
PAPER, 'The paper as . . . friend'. i.e. The paper, like the body of my friend, torn open
PARCEL, company, set
PARDON (n.), 'of pardon', to pardon me; (v.), remit (a penalty), IV i 364
PARROTS, 'like parrots', i.e. raucously (the parrot was proverbially a foolish bird)
PART, depart, II vii 77
PARTED, divided (see PROVERB), II ii 136
PARTI-COLOUR'D, of variegated colour
PARTS, qualities, accomplishments, I ii 38, II ii 167; tasks, IV i 92
PASSION, passionate outburst, II viii 12
PAST, 'past all saying nay', i.e. more forcefully than all my refusals
PATCH, fool (from 'Patch', apparently the name of a 'notable fool' of the time, or,

perhaps, from the Italian 'pazzo' = fool, or from the fact that a jester's clothes traditionally bore a patched design)

PATINES, dishes of silver or gold from which the consecrated bread of the Eucharist is served, (i.e., here, perhaps, small disks of gold and silver; see FLOOR)

PAWN'D, staked

PAY, 'pay him again', pay (it) him back again

PEEP, 'peep . . . eyes', i.e. look out through eyes half closed by laughter

PEIZE, (probably) weigh down, i.e. retard (or 'augment')

PEN, (innuendo)

PENNYWORTH, (i) small quantity, (ii) bargain

PENT-HOUSE, porch or projecting roof offering shelter from the weather

PERSUADED, pleaded

PETTY, i.e. smaller, less important, I i 12

PHOEBUS, Apollo, the classical sun-god

PICTURE, 'he is a . . . picture', i.e. he is handsome (only) in appearance ('picture' = mere appearance)

PIED, variegated in colour

PILL'D ME, stripped, peeled

PIRATES, (perhaps a pun: 'pir-rats')

PLACE, 'better place', higher rank

PLAY, make a wager, III ii 214; 'play the fool', (i) act foolishly, (ii) act the part of the fool (on the world's 'stage') (pun; see GRATIANO); 'play at dice . . . which', throw dice to decide which of the two

PLAY'D FALSE, (i.e. had extramarital sexual relations with)

PLEASE, 'If it please you to', i.e. Please

PLEASETH, it pleases

PLEASURE, give pleasure to me (i.e. by agreeing to help me), I iii 6

PLIES, repeatedly assails

POET, (perhaps Ovid, who, in his *Metamorphoses*, tells the story of the Thracian musician Orpheus, whose music had the power to charm even animals, trees, stones, and waters)

PORT, dignity, III ii 283; 'swelling port', splendid style of living

PORTIA, 'Cato's daughter, Brutus' Portia', Portia, the courageous and noble wife of Marcus Junius Brutus (conspirator with Cassius against Julius Caesar) and daughter of Cato Uticensis (an enemy of Caesar renowned for his moral rectitude). In Shakespeare's *Julius Caesar*, when her husband Brutus is

forced to flee from Rome after Caesar's assassination, Portia commits suicide by swallowing live coals)

PORTLY, stately, majestic (see SAIL)

POSSESS'D, informed, I iii 59, IV i 35; possessed of, IV i 384

POSSESSOR, see THIRD POSSESSOR

POST, swift messenger (the swiftest form of communication was by the 'post' messenger, who carried the mail because he travelled by means of relays of swift horses); (allusion to the fact that the 'post-horse' rider carried a horn), V i 46

POSY, a short motto (originally a line or verse of poetry inscribed within a finger-ring or on a knife)

POWERS, faculties

PRATING, chattering nonsensically

PRAY THEE, Please, I beg you

PRAYER, (i.e. his 'amen'), III i 18; 'that same prayer', (see the Lord's Prayer ('Forgive us our trespasses') and, perhaps, *Matthew* v 7 and *Ecclesiasticus* xxviii 2)

PREFERMENT, (being recommended for) advancement

PREFERR'D THEE, recommended you for advancement

PRESAGES, 'I have . . . presages me such', My mind so confidently predicts that I shall win such

PRESENCE, nobleness, dignity

PRESENT, ready, III ii 275; 'present sum', i.e. ready money

PRESENTLY, immediately

PREST UNTO, prepared, willing (perhaps 'bound') to do

PRETTY, (perhaps) artful, ingenious, II vi 37

PREVENTED, forestalled

PRINCIPAL, i.e. the original sum of the debt

PRIVY, private, secret

PRIZE, contest (at fencing, wrestling, etc.), III ii 141

PROCESS, (i) manner, (ii) legal process (probable pun)

PROCLAMATION, public advertisement (by means of a herald)

PRODIGAL, (see the parable of the Prodigal Son, *Luke* xv; see STRUMPET WIND)

PROFIT, improvement (in learning rather than wealth), II v 46

PRONOUNC'D, spoken, delivered, I ii 9

PROOF, 'childhood proof', (i) childish test or experiment, (or) (ii) experience of my youth

PROPHET, (allusion to the fact that Jews

102

conceded the prophetic, but not divine, status of Christ)
PROPORTION, harmony, balance, correspondence
PROVE, 'Prove it so', If it should prove so (see NOT)
PROVERB, i.e. 'He that hath the Grace of God hath enough', II ii 136
PUBLICAN, see FAWNING PUBLICAN
PUBLISH, make known
PUNY, childish, petty
PURCHAS'D BY THE WEIGHT, bought at so much an ounce (i.e. in the form of cosmetics)
PURSE (n.), wealth, II v 50; (v.), i.e. collect together in a bag, I iii 169
PURSUE, proceed with
PUTS, put, III ii 19
PYTHAGORAS, Greek philosopher and mathematician (fl. 540–510 BC) who propounded the doctrine of the transmigration of souls

QUAINT, ingenious, elaborate
QUAINTLY ORDERED, skilfully, elegantly, managed
QUALIFY, moderate
QUALITY, manner, III ii 6
QUARRELLING, 'quarrelling with occasion', i.e. disputing at every opportunity, (or 'being at odds with the matter in question')
QUESTION (n.), see USE, IV i 73; see HOLDS, IV i 167; see STAY, IV i 341; 'and I no question . . . sake', and I have no doubt that I shall be able to get money either on my credit as a business man ('trust') or for friendship's sake; 'in making question . . . uttermost', in doubting that I would do my utmost for you; (v.), dispute, IV i 70
QUESTIONLESS, undoubtedly
QUICKEN . . . HEAVINESS, enliven ('quicken') the sorrow to which he clings
QUIRING, singing in harmony
QUIT, (probably) remit (but perhaps 'have him pay')

RACE, herd, stud
RACK, instrument of torture which stretched the body (used to extort confessions from traitors which were often untrue), III ii 25
RACK'D, stretched
RAIL, chide
RAILS, utters abuse
RAISE, 'raise the waters', (either) stir things up, (or) induce tears

RANK, in heat, I iii 75
RASH-EMBRAC'D, rashly grasped
RASHER, slice of bacon
RATE, manner of living, I i 127; (i) amount (of interest which is charged), (ii) estimation, social respectability, I iii 40
RATED, reproved, reviled, I iii 102; valued, esteemed, II vii 26
RATING, valuing
READY, (used in replying to a call or summons = 'here'), IV i 2
REASON'D, talked
REASONING, 'this reasoning . . . me', this line of reasoning is not of a kind that will help me to choose
REASONS, reasonable statements, sensible ideas
REBELS, 'Rebels . . . years', i.e. Do you have sensual desires at your age (see FLESH AND BLOOD)
REDDEST, i.e. most courageous (red is traditionally the colour of valour)
REDEEM, rescue (see ALCIDES)
REDOUBTED, feared
REED, reedy (see BETWEEN)
REGARD, see WORTH
REGREETS, see SENSIBLE
REHEARS'D, specified, mentioned
RELATION, 'Hath full relation to', i.e. fully authorises
REMORSE, pity
REND APPAREL OUT, ruin your clothes by rough use
RENDER, perform, IV i 196; 'render . . . redoubted', make themselves feared
REPORT, see GOSSIP
REPROACH, (blunder for 'approach' = coming)
RESPECT, 'respect . . . world', concern for business affairs; 'Nothing is good . . . respect', i.e. Nothing is absolutely good, but only relatively good as modified by circumstances (or, perhaps, 'Nothing is good without the thought to make it so') ('respect' = reference to other circumstances)
RESPECTIVE, careful
REST (n.), see SET, II ii 93; (v.) remain, I i 152; 'Rest you fair', May you always have good fortune
REVERENCE, see DO, I i 13
RHENISH, red wine from the area of the Rhine (reputed to be of superior quality and potency to ordinary red wine)
RHEUM, spittle

RIALTO, a famous commercial district of Venice, the business exchange where important commercial transactions took place; also the marble bridge built across the Grand Canal

RIB, enclose

RIGHT, proper, V i 108

RING, (innuendo), V i 307

RIPE, that can have no longer delay, i.e. 'immediate'

RIPING, see STAY

ROAD, way, II ix 30; harbour, V i 288

ROADS, roadsteads, calm anchorages

ROMAN, 'ancient Roman honour', i.e. classical Roman ideal of stoical dignity, honour, and friendship

ROOF, i.e. roof of the mouth

ROUND HOSE, circular, puffed-out stockings or short breeches

RUDE, coarse, rough, II ii 166

RUIN, decay, III ii 174; 'ruin of', (i) refuse of, (ii) those who have been made destitute by

RULE, order

RUN, 'run . . . clock', i.e. are early

RUNAWAY, 'doth . . . runaway', i.e. is stealing swiftly away

SAD, melancholy, I i 1, I i 22, I i 47

SADNESS, melancholy, I i 6

SAIL, (i) sails, (ii) sailing, I i 9

SAME, 'is the same', i.e. is she, is the one, I i 119

SAND-BLIND, partly blind

SAV'D, 'sav'd by my husband', (compare *1 Corinthians* vii 14: 'the unbelieving wife is sanctified by the husband')

SAVING, 'saving your reverence', 'saving your worship's reverence', (conventional apologies before an expression which may be found to be offensive)

SAYING, being said, II ii 178; 'saying nothing', (compare *Proverbs* xvii 28: 'Even a fool, when he holdeth his peace, is counted wise')

SCANT, diminish (*see* EXCESS), III ii 112; make brief, V i 141

SCANTED, restricted, limited

SCAPE, escape

SCAPES, escapes, transgressions

SCARCE, (i) scarcely, (ii) (perhaps) stingy, parsimonious, II ii 116

SCARFED, i.e. decorated with flags (like a prodigal gallant wrapped in extravagantly ostentatious scarves; 'scarfed' could also mean

'with hull soundly jointed ('scarfed') together', in contrast to 'over-weather'd' of II vi 18)

SCHEDULE, paper with writing upon it

SCOTTISH, (possibly an allusion to an outbreak of disorder on the Scottish Border at the time when the play was written)

SCRUBBED, scrubby, stunted

'SCUSE, excuse

SCYLLA, (in Greek mythology, Scylla was a nymph whom Amphitrite changed into a female monster who lived on the Italian side of the Straits of Messina, had twelve feet, six heads (each on a long neck, and each armed with three rows of pointed teeth) and which barked like a dog. She preyed on passing mariners, who, in their efforts to avoid her, had to sail close to the whirlpool of Charybdis, at the other side of the Straits, and who thus ran the risk of being engulfed therein)

SEAL, agree, I iii 166; i.e. agree (in writing and affix my official waxen seal), I iii 147; ratify (as a legal document is ratified with a waxen seal), II vi 6

SEAL'D UNDER, see SURETY

SEARCH'D, probed (surgical term)

SEASON (n.), 'by season season'd are', are matured by favourable occasion

SEASON'D, gratified, IV i 97

SEASONS, tempers

SEAT, home

SEATED, see MEAN

SECOND, see DOWRY, III ii 95

SEED, 'seed of honour', offspring of nobility (quibble on 'seed' = (i) plant-seed, (ii) offspring; see GLEANED)

SEIZE, take possession of (legal term), IV i 348

SELF, same, I i 148

SEMBLANCE, exact image (*see* SOUL)

SENSE, 'in all sense', (i) in all reason, (ii) in every sense of the word

SENSIBLE, evident, intense, II viii 48; 'sensible regreets', tangible greetings (i.e. not words only; 'sensible' = evident to the senses)

SENTENCES, maxims

SERV'D FOR, see VENTURE

SERVE, allow, encourage, II ii 1

SERVES, see LEISURE, IV i 400

SERVITOR, servant

SET, 'set up my rest', finally, boldly resolved (phrase originally meaning 'stake everything' in the card game primero); 'set you forth', (i) serve you up, (ii) praise you highly (pun)

SEVER'D, separated

SHADOW, i.e. portrait (the mere shadow of substantial reality), III ii 127

SHADOW'D, 'The shadow'd . . . sun', (which is) the distinctively dark dress worn by the polished sun's servants ('shadow'd' = heraldic term for shaded, umbrated; 'livery' = distinctive uniform worn by the servants of a particular master)

SHADOWS, i.e. insubstantial, fleeting, delusions, II ix 66

SHADOW'S BLISS, i.e. a fleeting, insubstantial, happiness

SHAFT, arrow

SHALL, must, I i 116

SHIFT, see MAKE

SHOW, appear, IV i 191; 'show their teeth . . . smile', i.e. smile merrily

SHOWS (n.), 'to shows of dross', for tokens (or promise) of worthless rubbish ('dross'); (v.), i.e. symbolises, IV i 185

SHREWD, evil, unfortunate

SHRINE, image of a saint or god

SHRIVE ME, hear my confession (and impose penance upon me and grant me absolution)

SHYLOCK, (the origin of the name is obscure; it might have derived from 'Shiloh' of *Genesis* xlix 10, which a contemporary concordance glossed as 'mocked' or 'deceiving'; it might have overtones of the Hebrew 'Shallach' = cormorant (a word often used of usurers); it might be a form of 'Shelah', the father of Eber (i.e. Hebrew, see *Genesis* x 24); or it might come from a dialect term of contempt, 'Shullock', (derived from Old English) i.e. 'one who slouches about')

SIBYLLA, i.e. the prophetess Deiphobe of Cumae (to whom Apollo promised that she would live as many years as the grains of sand she was holding in her hand (see Ovid's *Metamorphoses* xiv))

SIGNIFY, make known, announce

SIGNIOR, gentleman of substance

SIGNIORS, see SIGNIOR

SILVER'D O'ER, i.e. silver-haired (and thus deceptively appearing to be wise)

SIMPLE, plain, unremarkable (ironic), II ii 146; uncomplicated, i.e. palpable, III ii 81

SIMPLICITY, see LOW SIMPLICITY

SINGLE BOND, (either) (i) technical term for a contract made without conditions (i.e. Shylock is playing down the significance of a bond which does, in fact, have conditions), (or) (ii) contract with Antonio's signature alone attached to it and without the signatures of other sureties)

SINGS, see ORB, V i 60; 'sings i'th'nose', i.e. drones with a sound like a nasal whine

SINS OF THE FATHER, i.e. consequences of, retribution for, the sins of their father (allusion to the Second Commandment in the *Second Prayer Book* (1552): 'and visit the sins of the father upon the children'; this was also a constant theme of Jewish theological history)

SIRRAH, form of address used to social inferiors

SISTERS THREE, see FATES

SITS, 'where sits the wind', which direction the wind is blowing from

SITTING, 'at a sitting', i.e. in a single moment

SLIGHTLY, easily

SLIPS OF PROLIXITY, lapses into prolixity, (or) words that are the product of prolixity, (or) wordy lies ('slips' = (i) cuttings from plants, (ii) faults, lapses, (iii) counterfeit coins)

SLUBBER, perform hurriedly or carelessly

SMACK, have a taste (i.e. was inclined towards lechery)

SMUG, neat, spruce

SNAKY, sinuous (with a suggestion of serpentine guile)

SO, see BUT, III ii 161; see DULL, III ii 163; provided (that), III ii 196, IV i 377; 'so following', i.e. so on, etcetera (see EAT), I iii 31; 'so far', see HOW, III ii 128; 'so you stand pleas'd withal', provided it pleases you; 'so please', if it pleases, IV i 2, IV i 375

SOFT, wait

SOLA, 'Sola . . . sola!', (perhaps hunting cries, or an imitation of the sound of a post-horn; see V i 46)

SOME, approximately an, II iv 26

SOMETHING, (often =) a little, somewhat; to some extent, I i 124; see SUM, III ii 158; i.e. particular coherent remark, shout, III ii 182

SOMETIMES, formerly

SONTIES, 'Be God's sonties', (probably) By God's saints (oath)

SOON, early, (this morning), II iii 5

SOOTH, truth; 'good sooth', indeed

SOPHY, King of Persia (regarded as the type of magnificence and power)

SORT (n.), considerable number, band, I i 88; (i) manner, way, (ii) casting, drawing, of lots, I ii 92; (v.), dispose, V i 132

SOUL, i.e. Bassanio, III iv 20

SPED, well-satisfied, (or) dealt with (in a bad sense)

SPEED, 'Which speed', Who are successful

SPEND BUT, only waste

SPICES, (i.e. her cargo of spices)

SPIRITS, (possible quibble, as 'spirits' were thought to have difficulty in travelling over water), II vii 46; mind, faculties of perception, V i 70

SPIT, spat

SPOILS, acts of plunder

SPOKE, spoken, III ii 179, IV i 197; 'spoke us yet', yet bespoken, given orders for

SPURN, kick

SPURN'D, kicked

SQUAND'RED, (unwisely) scattered

STAGE, (proverbial; see, e.g., As You Like It, II vii 139–166)

STAIRS OF SAND, (perhaps) steps cut in sand, (or) bulwark of sand

STAKE DOWN (gambling term) money to cover the bet paid down in advance (with innuendo on 'stake')

STAMP, 'the stamp of merit', a proper claim based on merit ('stamp' = official mark (certifying a document)

STAND (n.), standstill, V i 77; 'make a stand', wait; (v.), be, III ii 46; stand firm, wait, IV i 103; 'stand for sacrifice', am in a similar position as the sacrificial Hesione (see ALCIDES)

STANDING, stagnant

STANDS, remains, IV i 8

STATE, estate, property, III ii 261; 'his state', i.e. the grandeur of a 'substitute', V i 85

STAY, wait, II vi 59, II vi 63, V i 302; dalay, III ii 24; 'stay the very . . . time', wait for time to bring your business to ripeness and completion; 'stay here on', make a stand on, i.e. insist upon the fulfilment of; 'stay no longer question', do not tarry here to hear further argument

STAY'D FOR, awaited

STAYS, waits; 'stays without', is waiting outside

STEAD, assist, supply

STEAL, (but usury was often equated by contemporary thinkers with theft), I iii 85; 'steal your thoughts', gain possession of your thoughts, i.e. win your heart

STILL, (often =) always; continually, I i 17, III ii 74; 'live still', go on living

STILLNESS, see WILFUL STILLNESS, I i 90

STIRRING, happening, taking place

STOCKISH, 'so stockish', is so blockish, unfeeling

STOMACH, (i) appetite, (ii) inclination (pun)

STOMACHS, appetites

STOOD, depended, III ii 202; 'stood as fair', would stand as good a chance (play on 'fair' = not 'tawny')

STOP, staunch, IV i 253

STORE, wealth, I iii 48

STRAIGHT, immediately

STRAIN'D, constrained, compelled

STRANGE, distant, unfriendly (like a stranger), I i 67; 'more strange . . . strange apparent', more unusual, extraordinary . . . unnatural (see APPARENT)

STRANGER, alien, III ii 239

STRANGERS, aliens, III iii 27

STRATAGEMS, deceptive tricks

STREAKED, streaked in colour

STROND, strand, shore

STRUMPET WIND, i.e. dangerously fickle and deceptive wind (allusion to the strumpets (= prostitutes) courted by the Prodigal Son; see PRODIGAL)

STUBBORN, unyielding, hard-hearted

SUBSTANCE, solid, real, essence, i.e. verbal expression, III ii 127; the solid reality which casts the shadow, i.e. Portia herself, III ii 129; 'in the substance, Or . . . scruple', in the full amount ('substance') of a twentieth, or even a fraction ('division') of a twentieth of a 'scruple' (= a unit of weight equal to one twenty-fourth of an ounce; one twentieth of a 'scruple' = one 'grain')

SUDDENLY, i.e. without preparation, II viii 34

SUFFER, endure

SUFFERANCE, patient endurance

SUFFICIENT, (i) (legal term) adequate surety, (ii) substantial, well-to-do, I iii 14, I iii 21

SUFF'RANCE, endurance, suffering

SUIT, wooing, I ii 91; request, I iii 114, II ii 124; (i) request, (ii) livery, II ii 131; a request to make, II ii 162; see HABIT, II ii 186; request, wooing, II vii 73; legal claim, plea, IV i 62, IV i 172

SUITED, apparelled (what follows is a satire on the absurd internationalism of contemporary English gallants' fashions), I ii 65; adapted to suit the occasion (ironical), III v 56

SULTAN SOLYMAN, Suleiman II, the Magnificent (1496?–1566), a ruler of Turkey who conducted an unsuccessful campaign against

Persia in 1535. Morocco is either saying that he defeated Suleiman three times, or that he fought on both sides in the Persian/Turkish wars)

SUM, 'is the sum of something', adds up to something (she goes on to describe the 'something' more fully. Some editions read 'sum of nothing', i.e. 'adds up to nothing at all')

SUNDER, separate

SUP, take supper

SUPPOSED FAIRNESS, i.e. a supposedly beautiful woman

SUPPOSITION, 'in supposition', in doubt, uncertainty

SURETY, 'became his surety . . . for another', guaranteed the Scot's payment ('became . . . surety') and pledged himself ('sealed under') to pay the Englishman another blow (allusion to the constant promises of assistance which the French gave the Scots in the Scots' quarrels with the English)

SURFEIT, fall ill from excessive eating

SWAN-LIKE END, (the swan was thought to sing beautifully before dying)

SWAY, rule, power

SWAY'D, ruled, governed

SWEAR, 'swear upon a book', i.e. tell the truth (about the future. Launcelot plays upon the custom of placing the palm of the hand upon the Bible when taking an oath)

SWEAT AGAIN, sweated repeatedly

SWELLING, see PORT

SWORN, i.e. asked to give an answer to on oath, V i 301; 'dare be sworn for him', take an oath on his behalf

TABLE, a part of the palm of the hand (term from palmistry), II ii 145; i.e. food (pun), III v 52

TAINTED, infected with disease, sickly, IV i 114

TAKE, see BOND, I iii 22; 'you take my life . . . live', (compare *Ecclesiasticus* xxxiv 22: 'He that taketh away his neighbour's living, slayeth him')

TASTE, i.e. an inclination towards lechery (*see* SMACK), II ii 14

TELL, 'tell not me', i.e. don't trouble to tell me of this in reply to my question; 'tell every . . . ribs', (Launcelot's mistake for 'count ('tell') every rib I have with my fingers')

TEMPLE, (i.e. where he will take his oath)

TEN MORE, (*see* GOD-FATHERS)

TENDER, offer, IV i 204

TERM, 'term in gross', state in full

TERMS, (i) words, (ii) contractual arrangements, I iii 174; respect, II i 13; words, V i 205

THAT, i.e. Who, III ii 188

THE, 'the which', which; whom, IV i 347; 'the whilst', while

THEMSELVES, they themselves, II vi 37; 'be least themselves', i.e. falsify the inner reality

THERE, then, II viii 46

THEREFORE, therefor, for that reason (*see* SAYING), I i 96

THESE, 'of these', some men (*see* SAYING), I i 95

THINK, bear in mind, IV i 70

THIRD POSSESSOR, (allusion to *Genesis* xxvii. Isaac was Abraham's heir, and Esau should have inherited in turn from Isaac, thus becoming the 'third possessor'. However, Jacob's mother Rebeccah placed 'skins of kids' on Jacob's hands and neck, persuaded the blind Isaac that Jacob was his son Esau, and thus cheated Esau both of his inheritance and his father's blessing. (Shylock enjoys this tale of duplicity)

THISBY, (Thisbe, in classical myth the beloved of Pyramus, a Babylonian youth. Thisbe was to meet him at the white mulberry tree near the tomb of Ninus, but she was scared by a lion, and fled, leaving her veil, which the lion smeared with blood. Pyramus, arriving later and finding the blood-stained veil, concluded that she had been killed by the lion and committed suicide. When Thisbe returned, she found Pyramus's dead body and stabbed herself to death. The legend has it that their blood stained the white mulberry tree to its present colour)

THOUGHT, 'thought to', i.e. the capacity to think (which enables me) To, I i 36; 'a maiden hath . . . thought', a maiden can only speak exactly what she really feels (perhaps an allusion to the proverb 'Maidens should be seen and not heard')

THRIFT, (i) (mercenary) profit, (ii) success, I i 175; thriving, profit, I iii 45

THROSTLE, thrush

THROUGHFARES, thoroughfares

THROUGHLY, thoroughly, fully

THROW, (i) throw at dice, (ii) the fact that Hercules eventually flung Lichas to his death far out to sea (*see* LICHAS) (quibble)

TIME, life-time (perhaps 'youth'), I i 129

'TIS, it is; see OFFICE, II vi 43

TO, see LEARN, I i 5; 'to think', because he thinks, I i 40; 'to blame', too blameworthy, V i 166; see AN, V i 176

TONGUE, speech, II vi 27; see THOUGHT, III ii 8

TO-NIGHT, i.e. last night, II v 18

TOP, 'high top', topmast

TORCH-BEARERS, a common feature of masques

TOUCHES (n.), fingering or playing on a musical instrument, (i.e., here, 'notes')

TRADES, plies back and forth

TRAFFICKERS, (i) merchants, traders, (ii) i.e. merchant-vessels

TRAIN, retinue of attendants

TRAINS, see TRAIN

TRAJECT, i.e. ferry (from the Italian 'traghetto')

TREASON, see RACK, III ii 27

TRIAL, testing, IV i 161

TRICKSY, ingenious, clever

TRIED, see UNDERVALUED, II vii 53; 'Seven times tried . . . amiss', i.e. That judgement which never made a wrong decision is proven to be of the utmost purity ('tried' = of a metal, purified, refined by fire); 'tried this', i.e. purified, refined (the silver of this casket)

TRIFLE, waste time on trifles, IV i 293

TRIPOLIS, city port on the Mediterranean coast of North Lebanon

TROILUS, (mythical prince of Troy. He loved Cressid, daughter of the Greek priest Calchas. They vowed eternal love, but almost immediately an exchange of prisoners was arranged between the Trojan and Greek camps, and Cressid was exchanged for three Trojan princes. It was not long before, in the Greek camp, Cressid gave all her love to the Greek Diomed. As a consequence, the name 'Cressid' became synonymous with infidelity in love)

TROTH, good faith, honesty

TROYAN, Trojan

TRUST, see QUESTION, I i 185

TRUTH, see BEARS DOWN TRUTH, IV i 209; 'truth will . . . light', (proverbial)

TRY, 'try confusions', (Launcelot adapts the phrase 'try conclusions' = make experiments)

TUBAL, (name probably taken from Genesis x 2. A contemporary explained the name as meaning 'born worldly', or 'confusion', or 'slander')

TUCKET, distinctive series of notes on a trumpet

TURKS AND TARTARS, (i.e. unchristian heretics; see the Collect for Good Friday: 'Have mercy upon all Jews, Turks, Infidels, and Heretics')

TURN, change, III ii 248; 'turn into', become; 'turn to', (i) change into, (ii) copulate with (III iv 78; Portia reveals the pun, III iv 79f.); 'turn two mincing . . . stride', i.e. alter my gait so that my manly stride will then measure two of my present maidenly steps

TWAIN, two

'TWERE, it would be

TWINKLING, i.e. the time it takes to wink an eye

TWO-HEADED, see JANUS

TYRANNY, violence

UNBATED, undiminished

UNBURDEN, i.e. reveal, discuss

UNCHECK'D, unhindered, i.e. undenied

UNDERPRIZING IT, i.e. understating its beauty

UNDERTOOK, undertaken

UNDERVALU'D, see NOTHING, I i 165

UNDERVALUED, 'Being ten . . . gold', Being worth only one tenth as much as pure gold (In Shakespeare's day gold was worth ten times more than silver; 'tried' = refined, purified, tested by examination)

UNDONE, lost, ruined

UNFURNISH'D, i.e. without the other eye

UNHALLOWED, unblessed, unholy

UNHANDLED, untrained

UNLESS IN MIND, i.e. unless he is comforted by mental resolution, fortitude

UNMANNERLY, (perhaps pun on 'youth' = not yet a man, i.e. 'unmanly')

UNTHRIFT, prodigal

UNTREAD, retrace

UNWEARIED, i.e. most unwearied

UPON, see ADVANTAGE, I iii 65; into, onto, III i 39; by, in accordance with, IV i 104; 'Upon the fortune', i.e. Reliant upon the chance events; 'upon the hip', at a disadvantage (wrestling term; possibly an allusion to Jacob's wrestling with the angel described in Genesis xxxii 24ff.); 'My deeds upon my head', i.e. I ask no mercy for my deeds (perhaps with overtones of Matthew xxvii 25: 'His blood be on us and on our children')

URGE, offer, bring up, I i 144; 'urge the thing . . . ceremony', insist on being given something that was considered ('held') as a sacred or symbolic thing ('ceremony')

URGEST, vehemently pleadest for
USANCE, usury, I iii 40; interest, I iii 136
USANCES, usurous practices
US'D, accustomed
USE (n.), (play on 'use' = usury), I iii 108; habit, custom, IV i 263; 'in use', in trust (the precise meaning of this phrase is unclear: it could mean (i) (probably) that Antonio intends to administer his half of the estate, giving Shylock the legitimate profits until his death when the profits would become Lorenzo's; (ii) (less probably) that Antonio himself would enjoy the revenue; (iii) (less probably) that Lorenzo would enjoy the revenue, IV i 378; (v.), 'use it', make it my practice, I iii 65; 'use your pleasure', follow your own inclination; 'use question', debate
UTTERMOST, see QUESTION, I i 156

VAILING, lowering (as a sign of submission)
VANTAGE, opportunity
VARNISH'D, i.e. endowed with the outward appearance of nobility, II ix 49; 'varnish'd faces', i.e. (either) (i) painted faces, (or) (ii) masks
VASTY, vast
VENDIBLE, saleable (i.e. marriageable)
VENTURE, speculative commercial enterprise, I i 15; 'venture, sir, that Jacob serv'd for', commercial enterprise with an unpredictable outcome on which Jacob risked his time as a servant (or 'in which he played the part of a mere servant' ('serv'd for'))
VENTURES, (dangerous) speculative commercial enterprises
VENUS' PIGEONS, 'O ten times faster Venus' pigeons . . . unforfeited!', The doves of Venus fly ten times more swiftly to attend to a betrothal than they do to maintain a pledge of love already made ('obliged' = pledged; 'Venus' pigeons' probably alludes to the doves which were believed to draw the chariot of Venus (the classical goddess of love) through the air; perhaps 'pigeons' also = young lovers (often called 'doves'); 'pigeon' also = simpleton)
VERY, true, III ii 225; 'very Jew', a Jew indeed, in the fullest sense
VESTURE, clothing (see MUDDY)
VIA, Away, be off (used, for example, to encourage horses)
VIEW, i.e. (mere) external appearance, III ii 131
VILLAIN, villainous, base, II viii 4

VINEGAR ASPECT, bitter, obnoxious, appearance
VIRGIN TRIBUTE, see ALCIDES
VIRTUE, power, efficacy, V i 199
VISITED UPON, see SINS OF THE FATHER
VOICE, ''gainst . . . voice', however anyone else may vote
VOID, spit, I iii 112

WA HA, see SOLA
WAFT, beckoned
WAITING-MAID, superior female servant in personal attendance upon a lady
WAITING-WOMAN, female servant
WAKES, (perhaps) stays awake for watching or revelry
WANDS, slender sticks, saplings
WANTED, 'wanted the modesty', who would have been so lacking in moderation as
WANTON, untrained, V i 71
WANT-WIT, idiot, one who lacks wit or sense
WANTS, needs
WARRANT, guarantee
WARRANTY, authorisation (legal term = covenant or undertaking in contract)
WASTE, enjoyably spend, III iv 12
WATCH, wait, keep patient vigil, II vi 24
WAY, see SHOW, I i 55
WEALTH, welfare, V i 249
WEATHER, 'in the weather', i.e. in an exposed situation
WEEPING PHILOSOPHER, (i.e. Greek philosopher Heraclitus of Ephesus (c. 500 BC), who apparently wept when he beheld mankind's neglect of wisdom and good works for the pursuit of selfishness and transitory pleasures)
WELCOME, FROST, (inversion of the common saying 'Farewell, frost', used on parting with anything that was unwelcome)
WELL, 'well to live', with a good livelihood
WERE, (often =) (it) would be (a); 'were kindness', would indeed be kindness (i.e. benevolent and natural behaviour, if you really mean what you say); 'You were best', The best thing you could do would be; 'I were best', The best thing I could do would be
WETHER, sheep (a castrated ram)
WHEREOF, i.e. among which chests, I ii 26
WHETHER, 'Or whether', Or, III ii 117
WHICH, i.e. the 'table' and/or the 'man', II ii 145; Who, IV i 278, V i 115, V i 211
WHILES, while

109

WHO, (often =) whom; which, II vii 4; 'as who should say', as much as to say

WHY, 'Why, this is like . . . fair enough', Why, this is just as bad as it would be if one were to start mending roads in summer (when there is no need to mend them) and thus make them impassable (i.e.: for the wives to forsake their husbands and get lovers when their husbands were old and incapable would at least be understandable, but for them to forsake them when they are only just married would be absurd)

WILD (n.), wilderness, III ii 183; (adj.), unconfined, (or 'desolate'), V i 11

WILD-CAT, (i.e. which prowls by night and sleeps by day)

WILFUL, 'like a wilful youth', i.e. because I have behaved like a rash and self-willed youth; 'wilful stillness', self-imposed and persistent silence

WILL (n.), (i) desire, (ii) testament (pun), I ii 21; (v.), see NONE, III ii 102; 'Nor will not', see NOR, II i 43

WILLOW, (an emblem of forsaken love)

WIND (n.), (perhaps) breath, I i 22; (v.), 'To wind about . . . circumstance', To use a devious course of argument to win my love and persuade me (see CIRCUMSTANCE)

WINGS, bird's wings (i.e. the page's suit; pun on 'wing' = an ornamental flap above the upper end of a sleeve), III i 24

WISE, 'it is a wise . . . child', see IT

WISH, 'you can wish none from me', i.e. you have no need to be wished more joy by me (than you have already wished and obtained for yourselves)

WIT, wisdom, II i 18, IV i 141; intellectual ingenuity, II ix 81; ingenuity, II ix 98; 'To wit', That is, videlicet

WITH, by, III ii 119; 'with thy heels', see HEELS

WITHAL, therewith, II vii 12; with, III i 45; see SO, III ii 210; see COPE, IV i 407; in addition, IV i 445; 'I could not do withal', I could not help it

WITHOUT, outside, IV i 107

WIT-SNAPPER, nimble jester

WIVE, marry

WIVING, see HANGING

WOLF, (this may be a topical reference to the execution in June 1594 of a Portuguese Jew named Roderigo Lopez ('lupus' = 'wolf' in Latin) for an alleged attempt to poison Queen Elizabeth and Don Antonio, pretender to the throne of Portugal

WONDROUS, wonderfully, II viii 48

WONT, accustomed

WORD, 'fairer than that word', what is better still and more beautiful than that conventional epithet 'fair' implies

WORTH, 'Your worth . . . regard', i.e. I regard you as dear and valuable friends

WOULD, i.e. would like to borrow from him, I iii 60; would like to, I iii 111; do you want (see LORD), II ix 85; 'would almost damn . . . fool', would speak such nonsense that those who heard them would immediately call them fools and so risk damnation (allusion to Matthew v 22: 'And whosoever saith unto his brother, . . . Fool, shall be worthy to be punished with hell fire' (Geneva Bible)); 'would you', do you wish to ask of me, II ii 128

WREST ONCE, on this one occasion, forcibly subject

WRINKLES, see OLD

WRIT, wrote

WRONG ME, i.e. impute evil motives to me, I iii 165

WROTH, (= ruth) misfortune, grief

WROUGHT IN, laboured on (see THIRD POSSESSOR)

WRY-NECK'D FIFE, fife-player (or fife = small, shrill, flute-like instrument) with head twisted to one side

YET, up till now, II ix 91

YOUNG-EY'D, i.e. eternally keen-sighted

YOUNKER, young nobleman (some editions read 'younger' = younger son; compare the parable of the Prodigal Son, see, e.g., Luke xv)

YOUR, 'Your worship's . . . Launcelot', see LAUNCELOT

YOUTH, 'If that the youth . . . power', i.e. If my place in this household, still so new, gives me the right